Spiffy

Kitchen Collectibles

Brian S. Alexander

Published by

An F&W Publications Company

700 East State Street • Iola, WI 54990-0001
715-445-2214 • 888-457-2873
www.krause.com

Please call or write for our free catalog of publications. Our toll-free number to place an order or obtain a free catalog is 800-258-0929, or please use our regular business telephone 715-445-2214.

Library of Congress Catalog Number: 2003108018

ISBN: 0-87349-688-4

Editor: Tracy Schmidt
Designer: Jamie Griffin

Acknowledgments

The generous support of the following people made this book possible: Carol Alexander, who was there from the first page, thanks mom! My fabulous brothers and sisters, Jody, Greg, Doug, Diane, Shirley, Kent, and Jay—and my niece Dawn, thanks for being there for this one and the others. Eric Zorn and fellow members of his SIN support group, author Walter Oleksy and members in his writer's group, Paul Kennedy and Tracy Schmidt at Krause Publications. Bindy Bitterman at Eureka! Antiques, Evanston, IL for assistance with proofreading and a few wonderful finds! Patricia McDaniel at Storefront Antiques, Dublin, IN; Angie Wegner at Hawthorn Antique Mall & Gallery, Bristol, WI; and Marsha Brandom, cyber friend and supporter. Many of these people were there in the gray days of the project, where a change in the weather could (and sometimes did) affect the outcome.

Others helpful were John Leonard, Michelle Rioli, Tony Iuro, Matt Haylock, Robert Katzman at Magazine Memories, The Antique Market in Michigan City, IN; The Broadway Antique Market in Chicago; Douglas, Tim, Andy, and Tina. Assistance also came from Abbott Labs APCRU unit in Waukegan and their friendly staff, Osco film in Michigan City, Kinko's copies, U. S. Postal Service, the hundreds of Ebay sellers around the country (and world!).

Additionally I want to express my thanks to the many antiques malls, shops and shows tapped to assemble the items pictured in these pages, their locales follow. **Illinois:** Chicago, Wilmette, Gurnee, Volo, St. Charles, Rockford, Richmond, Hebron, Springfield, Wilmington, Des Plaines, Princeton, Sandwich, Grayslake. **Wisconsin :** Milwaukee, Racine, Kenosha, Bristol, Lake Geneva, Milton, Madison, Mount Horeb. **Indiana:** LaPorte, Chesterton, Valparaiso, Pines, Michigan City, Crown Point, South Bend, Pierceton, Lafayette, Delphi, Peru, Rochester, Boswell, Kentland, Fairmount, Lebanon, Indianapolis, Portland, Knightstown, Dublin, Richmond. **Michigan:** Niles, Lakeside, Union Pier, Sawyer, Allegan, Bangor. **Ohio:** Springfield, Dayton, and Columbus. **Iowa:** Des Moines.

A final thanks must be given to all those procrastinating cooks out there who never quite got around to using that what-cha-ma-callit!

Table of Contents

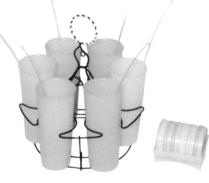

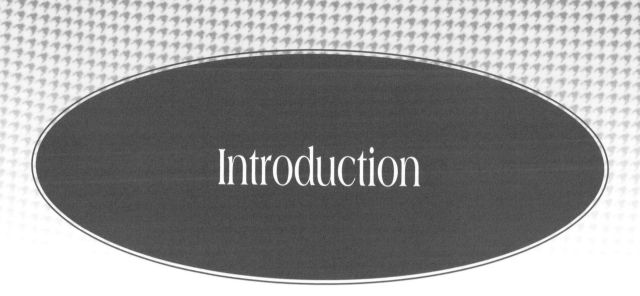

Introduction

I'm happy to present the numerous objects shown in *Spiffy Kitchen Collectibles* for your interest, amusement, and perhaps wonderment. Readers may question what constitutes a spiffy kitchen object as compared to an ordinary object. A somewhat nostalgic description, spiffy refers to something as being smart, bright, or having an enduring quality lacking in other objects. I took a cue from Hamilton Industries and the brightly striped picnic jug they called Spiffy in the 1950s, and tried to assemble an assortment of objects that represent a similar viewpoint.

Throughout the book, numerous period magazines, advertisements, and related materials are shown to help relate the objects pictured to the approximate era when they were produced. In many cases, these showcase the 'bright modern outlook' theme so prevalent in advertising images and product designs from the late 1940s to the 1960s. These optimistic images seem to convey the thought that yes, your life, or at least the chore at hand, could be better, easier, and faster if you would only use the product shown and not some lesser item available elsewhere.

All the items pictured are from my collection except as noted, and represent a broad spectrum of kitchen items and cooking activities. These include just about every task you would want to try to master in your kitchen of yesteryear. There are gadgets of all types, some of which question the intelligence of the user by their lack of necessity, and all sorts of accessories, sets, holders, and miscellaneous gizmos. Most of the items are non-electrical and small in scale; however, a few electrical and bigger items managed to find their way in as well.

The book tries to present examples that best show the various categories along with corresponding printed materials that help to explain how the products were used. Although only a fraction of the possible items that might fit the scope of the book are shown, the examples pictured help tell the story or history, if you will, of a time when elaborate meal preparation was a daily activity and convenience and prepackaged foods weren't so readily available.

Today, when big box stores have begun to transform the retail landscape, this book helps turn back the hands of that colorful kitchen clock to a not so distant past. It recalls a time when you could roam the aisles of your local store and perhaps find that special something you just couldn't do without (hopefully like this book). Happy Hunting!

Brian S. Alexander

Brian S. Alexander

Collecting
Kitchenware/Household Objects

The diverse area of kitchenware/household objects offers a world of collecting opportunities. Your interests may lead you to antique rarities more than one-hundred-years old or to items of more recent manufacture. Any and all territory should be considered fair game. As with other collectibles, your primary motivation should be your individual likes and preferences.

One question beginning collectors should ask, is how specialized they want their collections to be. Setting limits for your collecting range or territory is an important factor. You may be interested in true antiques for a display or you may want to concentrate on certain items such as molds, and have multiple examples that span a longer time period. Occasionally you will hear about a particularly interesting kitchenware/household object such as a heart-shaped ice-cream scoop from the 1920s, or an 1880s swan-shaped iron bringing thousands of dollars at auction. Many collectors marvel at these rarities, but can find a world of satisfaction collecting items in lower price ranges.

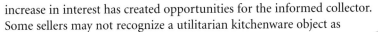

At the present time, there is a great deal of interest in kitchenware and related items from 35 to 60 years old; these objects rekindle old memories and represent a different, less-complicated era for many. As with other collectibles, this increased interest has created an upward curve in prices. Items that could be bought for a few dollars ten years ago are now generally worth five to ten times that amount, and higher-priced items have increased almost as much. This increase in interest has created opportunities for the informed collector. Some sellers may not recognize a utilitarian kitchenware object as being particularly valuable, or their interests may lie elsewhere. That's why the gizmo grandma had in her cupboard for decades might go for a fraction of its worth to an interested collector. But as a result of Internet auctions, many sellers are more informed and these types of bargains are harder to find.

Another factor affecting kitchenware items is the scarcity factor, as it relates to value. Few items from the last 50 years or so can be considered unique or one of a kind. However, it may happen that a certain vintage item, unused and in mint condition with its original label intact, and perhaps its original carton and price tag from the local store, becomes such a curiosity that its rarity and appeal to collectors is greatly enhanced. This can add appreciably to the item's value and price. If only one out of one hundred of these items still exists in this as-new condition, the scarcity curve is increased and the object, even if it was widely available when new, can now be considered scarce.

Collectors should let their interests guide them. If an object in mint as-new condition sufficiently adds to its worth to them, they can justify the added cost. In general, a vintage object that is mint and has its original graphically interesting box or packaging is worth about 25% more than a similar, nicely used example without its box.

Internet auctions have provided a way to discover more of these rarities and make them available for purchase. There are times when an object on screen becomes overwhelmingly irresistible to a collector. A word I made up to describe this appeal is Ebacious, a corny combination of Ebay and delicious. You know you've experienced an Ebacious object when you can't get it out of your mind, and your primary thoughts are focused on when the auction is scheduled to be over and what strategy might best ensure that you're the winning bidder. However, if someone else also finds the same object irresistible, the price of the item can easily escalate to unreasonable levels. Can you justify a hefty price tag for an item which might ordinarily sell for much less at a local antique mall or show? If so, proceed with caution, because it's likely a chance to acquire a similar object at a much lower price will come up, if you just exercise a little patience.

Another way a patient collector can acquire items at reasonable cost is to buy an object with a missing or broken part, usually at a considerable discount. In many instances the missing or broken piece can be replaced with an identical one, and the object becomes more valuable than the total cost you paid for it.

As with other collecting endeavors, in kitchenware it's foremost that the collector be happy with their collection. If an added benefit of collecting is the increase in value, fine, but potential value increases shouldn't drive your collecting. Another benefit for kitchen collectors is that many of the objects can still be used and function as well as, or better than, new items of the same type. With thorough cleaning and care, the object will retain its value and be an asset to your household rather than just a hands-off museum piece.

Fun-to-Collect
Spiffy Kitchen Products

Chapter 1

The World of Gadgets and How We Got There

A clear definition of what constitutes a gadget is somewhat elusive. According to a 1940s *Life Magazine* article, a gadget is a, "device for doing something that nobody knew needed doing until a gadget was invented to do it!" Although there may be some truth to this notion, the present day use of the word gadget has evolved through the years to encompass a broad array of items, mostly hand held, that help to perform a task.

In its broadest sense, even the simplest item such as a straight pin or a spoon could be described as a gadget. Familiarity with the item makes one forget that there was a time when even a spoon was a novel development needing training or repeated use to gain acceptance. In antiquity, a simple household spoon or knife was a prized possession, with the use of a fork for eating a relatively recent development stemming from France in the mid-eighteenth century. By the 1800s, knife, spoon, and fork utensil sets for eating became commonplace. This set the stage for the adoption of servers and other utensils.

In view of this history one might ask, how did the catchall gadget category as we know it today evolve? The first gadgets got their start in the era of Yankee ingenuity. In 1875, D. H. Goodell started a firm to make apple peelers and other devices out of cast iron. This company continued into the modern era with its core business intact. Others followed, including importers of overseas kitchen specialties such as Gustav Thurnauer. These businesses flourished on the East Coast where more distributors became involved and started selling similar items made at local sources. One of these source companies was the A&J Co. of Binghampton, N.Y., that made kitchen utensils and egg beaters. This created the manufacturing and distribution network that led the gadget and housewares industries into the twentieth century.

By the 1920s, gadgets had emerged as a distinct classification of housewares. In these earlier days of merchandising, it was common for stores to stash away smaller utilitarian items in drawers, limiting their access to customers. In the 1930s, an innovative east coast merchandiser, Michael Barry, and his family started selling gadget type items in bins along with illustrative placards that showed how they were to be used. This sales strategy helped invigorate the entire category by attracting the customer's attention and boosting sales. As more stores adopted this strategy, a separate sales area for gadgets became commonplace, giving the category a higher profile to customers and manufacturers. Along with this trend, the use of the word gadget evolved as a familiar way to describe these items.

In the 1940s, manufacturers began routinely mounting gadget-type devices on separate illustrative cards that could be wall or rack hung. The early versions of these used simple graphics and were somewhat utilitarian in appearance. This evolved by the 1950s into colorful pictures and graphics to help attract and hold the customer's attention. Sometimes the packaging used on these items seems more interesting than the objects themselves! Today, collectors look at a common kitchen gadget still attached to its original sales card or packaging as a seldom seen survivor, adding history, interest, curiosity, and in most cases a substantial increase in value.

Top Value Stamp Catalog. Cover picture shows a typically
well-dressed family doing some window-shopping, mid 1950s.
$15-$18

Metal Canister Set,
decorative kitchen gadget
design, marked
Weibro/Chicago. A
matching wastebasket was
also available, 1950s-1960s.

$40-$45

**Flaming Snowballs
Advertising Box,**
Heilemann Ice Cream,
Jefferson, WI. Coconut-
covered ice-cream balls
were a festive accessory for
that elegant 1950s-1960s
dinner party.

$10-$12

**Goodell White Mountain
Apple Parer,** Corer, and
Slicer, Goodell Co., Antrim,
NH. 1950s.

$40-$45

**Goodell White Mountain
Apple Parer,** Corer, and
Slicer, Goodell Co., Antrim,
NH, 1960s.

$30-$35

These are more recent
examples from a
company that began
producing cast-iron
peelers in 1875.

**Aluminum Measuring
Spoon Set,** accurate, handy,
four sizes on card, 1940s.

$15-$18

Mendets. "Mends all leaks
instantly, simply tighten.
Don't throw it away, mend
it with mendets," on card,
1940s, U S Standard.

$12-$15

New Meco Fiz-Kap, "Keeps
the pep in your beverages,"
on card, 1940s, Collette
Mfg. Co, Amsterdam, NY.

$12-$15

Cherry Pitter, metal, "For
fresh and preserved fruit,
Knocks out the pits," on
card, 1940s, Kenberry,
J.C.Brown Inc., Belleville,
NJ.

$8-$10

Chef's Triple Vegetable Cutter, metal, "Cut large and small strips," with insert card, 1940s, M&M Kitchen Aids, Chicago, IL.

$15-$18

Strawberry Huller & Pinfeather Picker, "Serves ice cubes, radishes, pickles, etc.," on card, 1941.

$8-$10

Quick Edge Sharpener, "For knives, lawn & garden tools," on card, 1940s, Kenberry, J C Brown Inc., Belleville, NJ.

$6-$8

Modern Egg Slicer, aluminum with stainless steel cutting wires, on card, 1940s, Household Specialties Co., Union, NJ.

$12-$15

Household Specialties Co., Union, NJ, French Fry Cutter and Garnishing Knife, stainless-steel blade with wood handle, on card, 1940s.

$15-$18

Kitchen Saw, "Cuts the hardest bones, a wonderful kitchen tool," on card, 1950, Kenberry, J.C. Brown, Inc., Belleville, NJ.

$12-$15

Speedee Chopper, on card, 1950s, Kenberry, J.C. Brown, Inc., Belleville, NJ.

$10-$12

Cookie & Pastry Tool, on card, 1956, Kenberry, J.C. Brown, Inc., Belleville, NJ.

$10-$12

Saturday Evening Post, February 28, 1955, with cover illustration by Stevan Dohanos.
The ladies are at a bridal shower admiring an eggbeater and other mid-fifties treasures.

$8-$10

Hostess Gadgets, for the Kitchen, five different tools, serving tongs, wire slicer, jar wrench, strawberry huller, and ejector fork, on card, 1930s, Kenberry, J.C. Brown, Inc., Belleville, NJ.

$22-$25

Punch-n-Cover, metal spike punches hole in evaporated milk can and acts as a cover, on card, 1950s, Mueller Mfg. Co., Greenville, MS.

$12-$15

Flexible Skillet Scraper, "Scraper bends to fit surface," on card, 1950s, McCormick Mfg. Co., Flora, IN.

$12-$15

Feemster's Marvel Peeler, "Quicker than a knife, Peels, Slices, Shreds," on card, 1950s, M.E. Heuck Co., Cincinnati, OH, either version.

$12-$15

Acme Rotary Mincer, stainless steel blade with wood handle, "For mincing, cutting noodles, etc.," in red or green with instructions, boxed, 1935.

$22- $25

Acme Garnishing Set, metal with wooden handles: garnisher, parer and corer, and slicer and shredder, in red or green, original price $1, boxed 1930s.

$25-$28

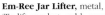

Em-Ree Jar Lifter, metal, 'To lift any hot, cold, open, or closed jar with safety," boxed 1940s, Emery & Sons Co., Detroit, MI.

$18-$22

Vapor-Vacuum Seal Opener, metal, "A quick easy way to open glass jars," on card, 1940s, White Cap Co., Chicago IL.

$12-$15

Jiffy Opener, metal, lid wrench, can punch, can opener, and lid lifter, on card, 1950s, Turner & Seymour Co., Torrington, CT.

$10-$12

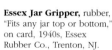

Grease-In Brush, styrene plastic and metal with integral brush, "Grease your pans—not your hands," boxed, 1950s, Hemco Products Co., Burbank, CA.

$15-$20

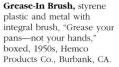

Essex Jar Gripper, rubber, "Fits any jar top or bottom," on card, 1940s, Essex Rubber Co., Trenton, NJ.

$12-$15

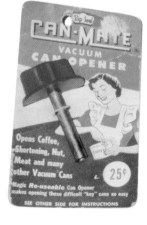

Krags Combination Jar Opener, metal, boxed, 1940s, Steel Products Co., Chicago, IL.

$8-$10

Can-Mate Vacuum Can Opener, metal with plastic handle, "Makes opening those difficult 'key' cans so easy," on card, 1950s.

$15-$18

Bottle Cappers, Slip Seal Co., Long Beach, CA. "Save the sparkle and you save the flavor," on card, 1950s-1960s, Acme Metal Goods Co., Newark, NJ.

$10-$12

Percomatic Baster, aluminum, "It's automatic, for roasts, chicken, ham, etc.," boxed, 1949.

$12-$15

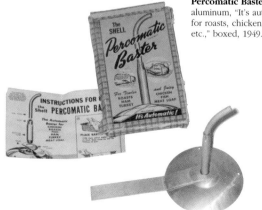

Magic Cream Remover Siphon, aluminum, "Removes cream, starts and stops itself," boxed, 1940s-1950s, Paul V. Shell Co., Kansas City, MO.

$12-$15

Get The "Thing-A-Ma-bob" That Does

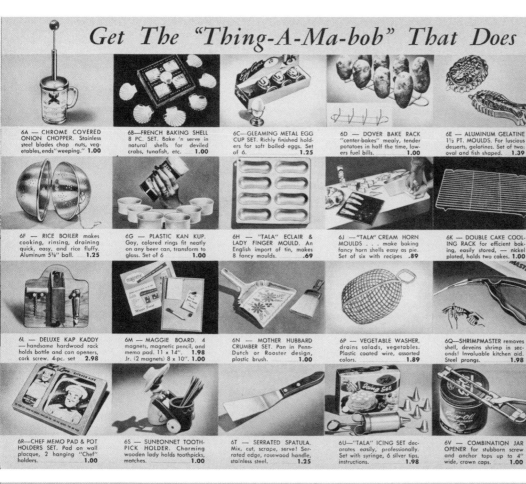

6A — CHROME COVERED ONION CHOPPER. Stainless steel blades chop nuts, vegetables, ends "weeping." **1.00**

6B—FRENCH BAKING SHELL 8 PC. SET. Bake 'n serve in natural shells for deviled crabs, tunafish, etc. **1.00**

6C—GLEAMING METAL EGG CUP SET. Richly finished holders for soft boiled eggs. Set of 6. **1.25**

6D — DOVER BAKE RACK "center-bakes" mealy, tender potatoes in half the time, lowers fuel bills. **1.00**

6E — ALUMINUM GELATINE 1½ PT. MOULDS. For luscious desserts, gelatines. Set of two: oval and fish shaped. **1.39**

6F — RICE BOILER makes cooking, rinsing, draining quick, easy, and rice fluffy. Aluminum 5⅜" ball. **1.25**

6G — PLASTIC KAN KUP. Gay, colored rings fit neatly on any beer can, transform to glass. Set of 6 **1.00**

6H — "TALA" ECLAIR & LADY FINGER MOULD. An English import of tin, makes 8 fancy moulds. **.69**

6J — "TALA" CREAM HORN MOULDS . . . make baking fancy horn shells easy as pie. Set of six with recipes **.89**

6K — DOUBLE CAKE COOLING RACK for efficient baking, easily stored, — nickel plated, holds two cakes. **1.00**

6L — DELUXE KAP KADDY — handsome hardwood rack holds bottle and can openers, cork screw. 4-pc. set **2.98**

6M — MAGGIE BOARD. 4 magnets, magnetic pencil, and memo pad. 11 x 14". **1.98** Jr. (2 magnets) 8 x 10". **1.00**

6N — MOTHER HUBBARD CRUMBER SET. Pan in Penn-Dutch or Rooster design, plastic brush. **1.00**

6P — VEGETABLE WASHER, drains salads, vegetables. Plastic coated wire, assorted colors. **1.89**

6Q—SHRIMPMASTER removes shell, deveins shrimp in seconds! Invaluable kitchen aid. Steel prongs. **1.98**

6R—CHEF MEMO PAD & POT HOLDERS SET. Pad on wall placque, 2 hanging "Chef" holders. **1.00**

6S — SUNBONNET TOOTH-PICK HOLDER. Charming wooden lady holds toothpicks, matches. **1.00**

6T — SERRATED SPATULA. Mix, cut, scrape, serve! Serrated edge, rosewood handle, stainless steel. **1.25**

6U—"TALA" ICING SET decorates easily, professionally. Set with syringe, 6 silver tips, instructions. **1.98**

6V — COMBINATION JAR OPENER for stubborn screw and anchor tops up to 4" wide, crown caps. **1.00**

The Job - A Few of Our Many H & P Gadgets

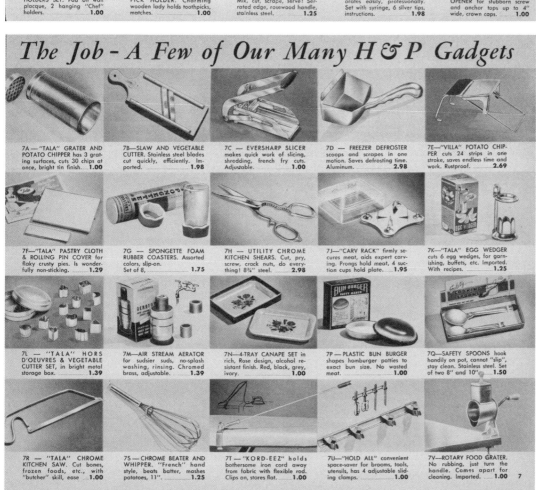

7A — "TALA" GRATER AND POTATO CHIPPER has 3 grating surfaces, cuts 30 chips at once, bright tin finish. **1.00**

7B—SLAW AND VEGETABLE CUTTER. Stainless steel blades cut quickly, efficiently. Imported. **1.98**

7C — EVERSHARP SLICER makes quick work of slicing, shredding, french fry cuts. Adjustable. **1.00**

7D — FREEZER DEFROSTER scoops and scrapes in one motion. Saves defrosting time. Aluminum. **2.98**

7E—"VILLA" POTATO CHIPPER cuts 24 strips in one stroke, saves endless time and work. Rustproof. **2.69**

7F—"TALA" PASTRY CLOTH & ROLLING PIN COVER for flaky crusty pies. Is wonderfully non-sticking. **1.29**

7G — SPONGETTE FOAM RUBBER COASTERS. Assorted colors, slip-on. Set of 8. **1.75**

7H — UTILITY CHROME KITCHEN SHEARS. Cut, pry, screw, crack nuts, do everything! 8¾" steel. **2.98**

7J—"CARV RACK" firmly secures meat, aids expert carving. Prongs hold meat, 4 suction cups hold plate. **1.95**

7K — "TALA" EGG WEDGER cuts 6 egg wedges, for garnishing, buffets, etc. Imported. With recipes. **1.25**

7L — "TALA" HORS D'OEUVRES & VEGETABLE CUTTER SET, in bright metal storage box. **1.39**

7M—AIR STREAM AERATOR for sudsier suds, no-splash washing, rinsing. Chromed brass, adjustable. **1.39**

7N—4-TRAY CANAPE SET in rich, Rose design, alcohol resistant finish. Red, black, grey, ivory. **1.00**

7P—PLASTIC BUN BURGER shapes hamburger patties to exact bun size. No wasted meat. **1.00**

7Q—SAFETY SPOONS hook handily on pot, cannot "slip", stay clean. Stainless steel. Set of two 8" and 10". **1.50**

7R — "TALA" CHROME KITCHEN SAW. Cut bones, frozen foods, etc., with "butcher" skill, ease **1.00**

7S — CHROME BEATER AND WHIPPER. "French" hand style, beats batter, mashes potatoes, 11". **1.25**

7T — "KORD-EEZ" holds bothersome iron cord away from fabric with flexible rod. Clips on, stores flat. **1.00**

7U—"HOLD ALL" convenient space-saver for brooms, tools, utensils, has 4 adjustable sliding clamps. **1.00**

7V—ROTARY FOOD GRATER. No rubbing, just turn the handle. Comes apart for cleaning. Imported. **1.00**

House Furnishings Review contained this picture of Michael Barry and his New York Gadget Shop in the early 1930s.

House Furnishings Review published this photo of a typical gadget bar inside a hardware store in the late 1940s—early 1950s.

According to the original caption for this picture appearing in *House Furnishings Review,* "farming people are more gadget conscious than city folks," as they stand before an early 1950s gadget bar.

Housewares catalog page from the *Acebi Stamp Catalog,* mid 1950s.

$12-$15

Gadgets Galore!

Make light work of everyday tasks

MIRRO COOKIE PRESS... holds enough dough for 80 cookies! Discs and tips included enable you to make a variety of fancy pastries. 3" diam. barrel. Has "Easy-Grip" handle.   **NO. 505-131B**

DAZEY ICE CRUSHER. Grinds ice fine, medium or coarse at just a turn of the handle. Stainless steel mechanism, white enameled body. Wall bracket included   **NO. 504-035B**

RIVAL ICE-O-MAT. Set dial, turn handle...and ice is crushed fine, medium or coarse! Plastic cup catches crushed ice. White enameled; chrome trim ...   **NO. 504-118B**

"TILT TOP" JUICE-O-MAT. One turn of handle raises, tilts top. Half turn gets all the juice from fruit! Aluminum drain-cup pitcher. Red enameled with chrome trim   **NO. 504-142B**

DOZEN DISH TOWELS. Bleached, ironed, hemmed...these sturdy sugar and flour sacks do a marvelous job on dishes and glassware! Dozen (each 17x30")   **NO. 502-567B**

DAZEY MAGNETIC CAN OPENER. Cuts out entire top of can; magnet keeps it from falling. Swings to wall. Red/chrome   **NO. 504-019B**
Without magnet   **NO. 504-027B**

BISSELL "SWEEPMASTER." Smaller, lighter, sweeps full width. Goes up to baseboards, under furniture; adjusts to rug thickness. Nylon bearings; built-in brush cleaner   **NO. 502-674B**

ROAST MEAT THERMOMETER. Takes all the guesswork out of roasting! Meat temperatures on enameled scale; pointed bulb with chrome guard. Easy to clean. 7¾"   **NO. 271-437A**

Self-cleaning nylon bristles

Suds or clear... at fingertip control

BORG BATH SCALE. Streamlined, wafer-thin...yet it accurately weighs up to 250 lbs. "Binocular" dial; broad rubber topped platform. White with chrome   **NO. 502-435B**

JET BRUSH DISHWASHER. Push-button action shoots liquid detergent (in plastic handle) down to nylon bristles ...scrubs dishes clean! Built-in scraper. 9½" long   **NO. 502-625B**

COSCO DELUXE STEP STOOL... a comfortable chair that becomes a safe, sturdy ladder when steps are swung out from under the seat. Definitely one of the handiest pieces of furniture you could have in your kitchen... you'll be amazed at how convenient it is at meal preparation time, on ironing day, or when there's a high shelf to be reached.
Handsome too, in gleaming chrome with foam rubber seat and padded back rest covered in bright colored Tuflex plastic. Swing-away steps with rubber treads. Seat 24" high. Specify; Choice of Red, Yellow, Gray or Green upholstery   **NO. 508-002D**

ALUMINUM OVEN-SHOVEL. Takes pies, cakes, out of the oven; lifts off baked potatoes; slips franks off the grill. And you won't burn your fingers. Stain proof   **NO. 504-290B**

STAINLESS STEEL BASTER. Drains grease from gravy, skims milk; injects special seasonings into meat or fowl. Easy to use; easy to clean. Rubber bulb   **NO. 505-297B**

21

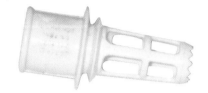

Juistractor, styrene plastic, "Easy to use, Gets all the juice," boxed, 1950s, Popeil Bros., Chicago, IL.

$10-$12

Citrex Fruit Juice Extractor, styrene plastic, boxed, 1950s, The Juice Extractor Co., Pittsburg, PA.

$10-$12

Nut Cracker, Nut Pick Set, metal, boxed, 1950s, H.M. Quackenbush Co., Herkimer, NY.

$15-$18

Rocket Nut Cracker, metal with a wood base, "America's finest nut cracker," boxed, 1950s, Arthur W. Reed Co., Little Rock, AK.

$22-$25

Flame Minder, metal, "Makes every pot a double boiler," boxed 1950s, Kitchen King.

$15-$18

Dubuque, IA, Op-N-Seal, metal, "The all around lifetime utensil," on card, 1950s, Op-N-Seal Sales Co.

$15-$18

Mystic "Grip Disc," rubber sheet, "If it is tight—grip disc is right," in sleeve, 1950s promotional piece.

$12-$15

Handi Spout, styrene plastic, "For milk, cream, etc. No more broken fingernails," on card, 1940s-1950s, Plastic Metal Mfg. Co., Chicago, IL.

$12-$15

Can Master Pouring Spout, plastic with stainless steel piercer, "Opens and pours,'" on card, 1950s, Cornwall Corp., Boston, MA.

$15-$18

Liqui-Pour, styrene plastic with rubber seal, "Opens, Pours, Stores, The greatest invention since the can opener," on card, 1972, Business Builders Intl., Chicago, IL.

$10-$12

Tongs, chrome plated, "All purpose, Sturdy, Safe," on card, 1950s, Vaughan Mfg. Co., Chicago, IL.

large	**$15-$18**
small	**$10-$12**

EKCOLINE Kitchen Tools

TO MAKE WORK FUN AND BRIGHTEN UP YOUR KITCHEN

BARGAIN!

7-PIECE SET (INCLUDING RACK) $6.04 VALUE . . . ONLY $5.49

Available with Red, Yellow, Blue or Green Handles

INDIVIDUAL TOOLS, 69¢ (LADLE, MASHER, STRAINERS, 79¢ and 89¢)

Save Wear and Tear on Your Hands With These Smooth New Tools

These new Ekcoline Kitchen Tools have scientifically designed "wing grip" handles that won't roll or slip in your hands.

And they're easier to use because better balanced. And stronger because precision made of resilient hardened stainless steel.

Get Ekcoline Kitchen Tools and be proud of your kitchen. Take advantage of the special bargain set offer while they last. Find them at good hardware, department, or appliance stores . . . wherever good housewares are sold.

NO OTHER KITCHEN TOOL OFFERS ALL 6 FEATURES

1. "WinGrip" Polished Plastic Handles won't slip or roll in hand.
2. Electro-Welded Joints— Cannot Collect Dirt— Stronger.
3. Resilient Hardened Stainless Steel.
4. Lustrous Mirror Finish Blades and Bowls.
5. Heat Bonded Shafts—Can't Pull Out of Handles.
6. Convenient Hang-up Holes in Handles.

EKCOLINE Kitchen Tools Precision Made by EKCO

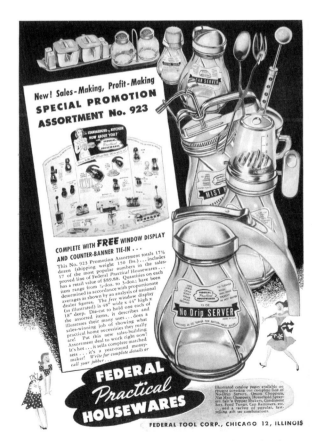

New! Sales-Making, Profit-Making SPECIAL PROMOTION ASSORTMENT No. 923

COMPLETE WITH FREE WINDOW DISPLAY AND COUNTER-BANNER TIE-IN . . .

This No. 923 Promotion Assortment totals 17½ dozen (shipping weight 150 lbs.) . . . includes 17 of the most popular numbers in the sales-proved line of Federal *Practical Housewares* . . . has a retail value of $89.88. Quantities on each item range from 1-doz. to 3-doz. have been determined in accordance with proportionate averages as shown by an analysis of national dealer figures. The *free* window display (as illustrated) is 48" high x 44" wide x 18" deep. Die-cut to hold one each of the assorted items, it describes and illustrates their many uses . . . does a sales-winning job of showing what practical home necessities they really are! Put this new sales-building Assortment deal to work right now! It's hot . . . it sells complete matched sets . . . it's a year-round money-maker! *Write for complete details or call your Jobber* . . .

No Drip SERVER

FEDERAL Practical HOUSEWARES

Illustrated catalog pages available on request covering our complete line of No-Drip Servers, Onion Choppers, Nut Meat Choppers, Household Sprayer, Salt 'n' Pepper Shakers, Condiment Sets, Food Tongs, Cap Removers, etc., and a variety of popular, fast-selling assortment combinations.

FEDERAL TOOL CORP., CHICAGO 12, ILLINOIS

Federal Practical Housewares ad showing their 1940s product line and a store window display, *House Furnishing Review,* July 10, 1948

$2-$5

Ekcoline Kitchen Tools ad from the early 1950s.

$3-$5

8-A MIRRO-MATIC PRESSURE COOKER. High polish solid aluminum, 8 qt. .... **6 Books**
4 qt. .... **4 Books**

8-B PEMSCO PIE AND CAKE CARRIER. Metal tray, decorated cover. Two decks, 12″ wide. Wire carrier holds securely .... **1 Book**

8-C NATIONAL SLICING MACHINE. 6½″ blade. Slices thin to ¾″ thick. .... **5 Books**

8-D MIRRO COPPER-TONE MOLD SET. Tarnish-proof, 5 popular molds for salads and desserts. .... **2 Books**

8-E PYREX OVEN-PROOF MIXING BOWL SET. 4 nested bowls, assorted colors .... **1 Book**

8-F TRANSPARENT LOCK-LIFT CAKE COVER. Poly-ethylene top, 22″ styrene tray. Red or yellow. .... **1 Book**

8-G SWING-A-WAY ICE CRUSHER. Table-type portable. Holds 2 trays of crushed ice. 5-year guarantee .... **3 Books**

8-H FRENCH FRY CUTTER. Rustproof metal, cuts whole potato at one time .... **1 Book**

8-J SWING-A-WAY WALL TYPE CAN OPENER. Cadmium plated. Holds can while rim is smoothly cut and turned .... **1 Book**

8-K SWING-A-WAY AUTOMATIC CAN OPENER. Magnetic lid lifter, assorted colors .... **2 Books**

8-L REGAL COVERED FRY PAN. Aluminum, ano-dized copper-aluminum cover. .... **2 Books**

8-M REGAL 5½ QT. DUTCH OVEN. Aluminum waterless cookware, anodized copper-aluminum cover. .... **2 Books**

8-N REGAL 3-QT. COMBINATION COOKER. Alumi-num waterless cookware, anodized copper-aluminum cover .... **2 Books**

8-O REGAL 2-QT. SAUCEPAN. Aluminum waterless cookware, anodized copper-aluminum cover. .... **2 Books**

8-P MIRRO COMBINATION COOKER. 3-Qt. alumi-num, weighted cover .... **1 Book**

8-Q ENTERPRISE ALUMINUM PERCOLATOR. 8 cup, high quality, bakelite handle .... **1 Book**

8-R BRIDGEPORT "PRIDE AND JOY" SET. Stain-less steel copper core, 11″ skillet, 2-qt. casserole, 2½-qt. saucepan and warmer .... **9 Books**

8-S COSCO DELUXE STEP STOOL. Rubber-treaded, "swing-away" steps, chromium plated legs, upholstered padded seat and back. Assorted colors .... **5 Books**

8-T COSCO HI-YOUTH CHAIR. Duran plastic padded seat and back, tubular chrome frame. Assorted colors .... **5 Books**

9-A MASTERWARE ALL CHROME CANISTER SET. 4-piece, space saving, stackable; 5 lbs. sugar, flour; 1½ lbs. coffee, tea.

Catalog pages from the *Holden Trading Stamp Catalog,* mid 1950s.

$12-$15

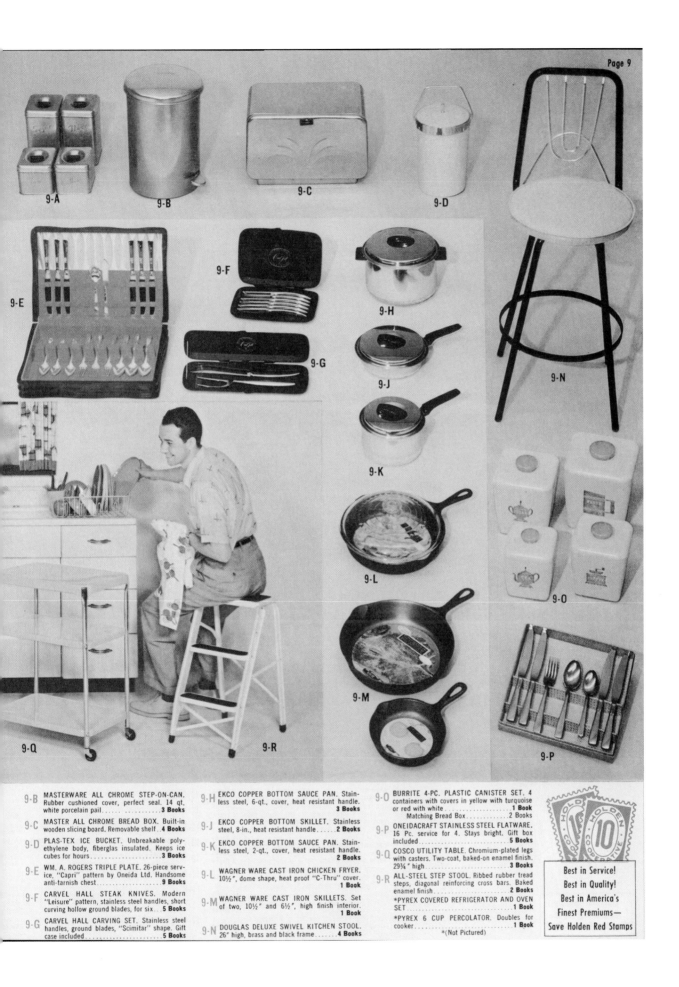

9-A

9-B

9-C

9-D

9-E

9-F

9-G

9-H

9-J

9-K

9-N

9-L

9-O

9-M

9-Q

9-R

9-P

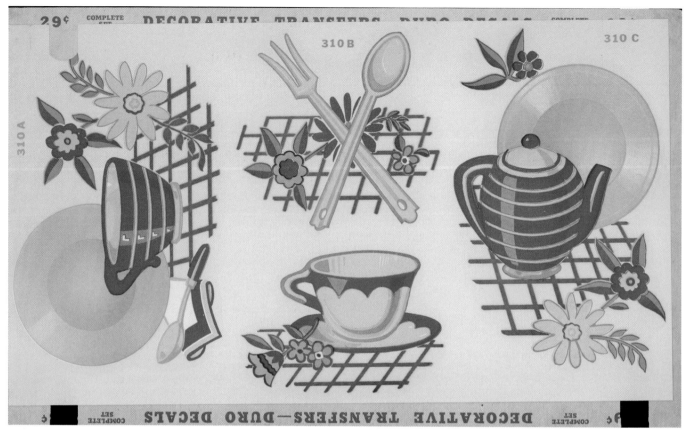

Colorful Decals having a kitchen or gadget theme make a fun addition to kitchen collections.
Duro Decals with a streamlined kitchen illustration on reverse, 1940s-1950s.

$12-$15

Meyercord Decals with collages of kitchen items, "For a colorful home," 1940s-1950s.

$10-$12

Chapter 2

Ekco Products Co.

According to a 1920s' sales letter from the Edward Katzinger Co. (Ekco is their shortened name), they were the largest company in the tin pan business and in an age of specialization excelled because they made, "nothing but tin pans." This strategy would change with the acquisition of over ten various companies through the years, and the restructuring around the Ekco name. By the 1950s, they were heralding themselves as, "the greatest name in housewares," and made just about every imaginable kind of pan, utensil, gadget, or what have you.

All this activity had humble beginnings during the 1880s, when the newly immigrated Edward Katzinger, resettled in Chicago. Katzinger was, by trade, a tinsmith and mechanic. He quickly set up a shop to make tin pans for commercial bakeries. By 1916, Edward's son Arthur had joined the company. In the late 1920s, after a series of moves, expansions, and a company acquisition, they were the leading tin pan maker for the commercial and consumer markets.

By the 1930s, kitchen tools and utensils were added to the line after they acquired the A&J company. In 1939, son Arthur took over the operation and changed his name to Arthur Keating. From the 1940s on, there were additional acquisitions including: a cutlery firm, a metal stamping plant, a wood products company, and a plastics molder. All were combined under the Ekco banner in 1946.

Arthur Keating led Ekco through the 1950s & 1960s and further expanded into such divergent product categories as shoe trees, garment stretchers, bathroom fixtures, and storage lockers. In 1965, American Home Products acquired Ekco, and Arthur Keating died in 1967. His successes as a businessman are evident as the company continues its operation into the twenty-first century.

A number of products made by Ekco are of particular interest to collectors today. Nearly everyone over the age of 40 has had some personal interaction with a vintage Ekco kitchen tool or gadget. Kitchen collectors everywhere love the finely crafted and durable Ekco tools with their colorful handles. Most items were made in red, yellow, turquoise, pink, and black. Today, red commands the most interest with pink, yellow, and turquoise not far behind. Black is least preferred, so that a luxury stainless steel tool in black is less desirable than a budget version in red. This same trend is prevalent in other items for the kitchen, such as beaters.

In addition to utensils, Ekco made many other kitchen items and accessories, including rolling pins, bakeware, and an extensive selection of gadgets. In a recent Internet auction a 1950s aluminum rolling pin mint in the box would set you back over $50. But regardless of where an object turns up, collectors can have a veritable field day without having to go beyond the Ekco name.

Magic Cake Pan Set, boxed, 1920s-$1930s, Edward Katzinger Co.

$30-$35

Ovenex Magic Cake Pan Set, "So easy to make this unusual two-tone cake," boxed, 1950s, Ekco Products Co.

$22-$25

Ice Box Cookie Moulds, "A favorite at parties and teas," boxed 1930s, Edward Katzinger Co.

$30-$35

Ekco Pastry Kneader, 1940s.

$8-$12

Ekco Batter Whip, 1940s.
$12-$15

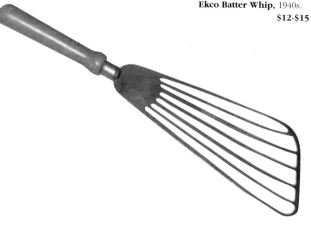

Swans Down Cake Pan, "Swans Down cake flour makes better cakes," 1920s.

$25-$30

Swans Down Cake Pan, (side view), Pat. Dec 18-23, 1920s, E. Katzinger Co.

$25-$30

Upside Down Cake Pan with Label, 1950s, Ekco Products Co./Ovenex.

$25-$28

EKCOLOY® BAKEWARE

with sparkling new labels to sell faster

Ekcolay Bakeware product catalog, "women prefer Ekcolay 2 to 1," 1950s. Catalog value: **$15-$18**

EKCO EGG BEATERS

TO MATCH EKCO KITCHEN TOOLS

A complete line of budget priced egg beaters made to retail at the fastest selling price points. Each one is a quality Ekco product . . . the finest in its price class.

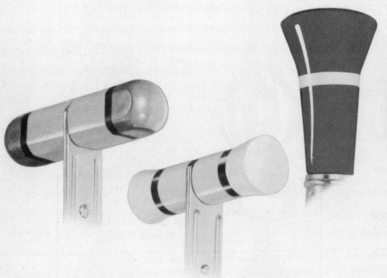

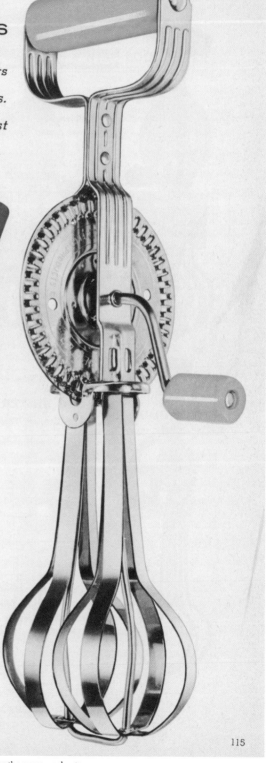

These beaters are available in a variety of handle styles and most come in colors to match Ekco kitchen tools. Sell them as a separate egg beater line or as companion items to Ekco kitchen tools.

115

Eggbeaters from a 1957 Ekco Products catalog. Over the years eggbeaters were made in a variety of styles and price ranges. Versions with eight stainless steel blades were considered a step up from plated eight or four-blade models.

Spring Form Cake Pan, "For sponge cake, sunshine cake, fruit cake, etc.," with label, 1950s, Ekco Products Co./Ovenex.

$25-$28

Ekco/Ovenex Baking Pans, Ekco acquired the Republic Stamping Co., and their Ovenex brand in 1952. Heart cake pans with sunburst finish, lightly used, 1950s.

$15-$18

Ekco/Ovenex Baking Pans, loaf pans, lightly used, 1950s.

$8-$12

Ekcoloy Silver Beauty Cookie Sheet, with pull-n-hang handle, and **Ekcoloy Silver Beauty Refrigerator Cake Pan.** Both with label 1959, Ekco Products Co./Autoyre Div.

$18-$22

A&J Egg Beater, with 1923 patent date, this model was made at A&J prior to being acquired by Ekco in 1929. Examples with little paint loss or other signs of wear command top prices: Left: red handle, Ekco/A&J Egg Beater.

$22-$25

Right: green handle, 1930s.

$18-$22

Ekco non-spatter Egg Beater and Bowl Set, (quart), A&J with 1923 patent date.

$40-$45

Ekco Non-spatter Egg Beater and Bowl Set, wire loop handle version (pint).

$35-$40

Ekco Masher Strainer,
1940s-1950s.

$18-$22

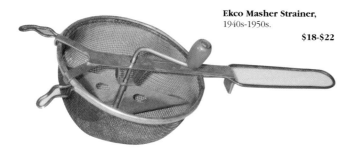

Ekco Eggbeaters, red with
white stripes, flared "T"
handle with high-speed
center drive, Ekco/USA,
1950s.

$18-$25

Ekco Eggbeaters, yellow
and white with spade
handle and high-speed
center drive, Ekco/A&J
1950s.

$18-$25

Ekco Eggbeaters, black
with spade handle, stainless
steel blades and original
insert card, Ekco/A&J, 1950s.

$22-$25

Ekco Rhythm Beater,
black plastic handle, boxed,
1950s.

$22-$25

Eggbeater, Flint, with
rhythm beaters, coordinates
with flint stainless steel
utensils, 1950s.

$15-$22

**Ekco/A&J Natural Finish
Utensils,** unused with
labeling intact, 1940s.

$15-$18 each

Ekcoline Utensil Set,
seven pieces with red and
white plastic handles,
boxed, unused, 1940s-
1950s.

$95-$125

A number of matching
utensils could be added to
the basic sets, which were
also made in yellow, green,
and blue, individual pieces.

$15-$18

NOW! THE FLINT "BEST"
WITH **NEW RHYTHM BEATERS**

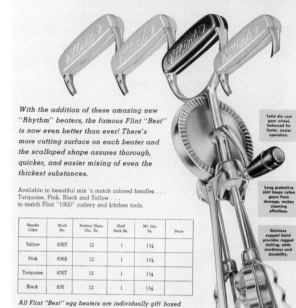

With the addition of these amazing new "Rhythm" beaters, the famous Flint "Best" is now even better than ever! There's more cutting surface on each beater and the scalloped shape assures thorough, quicker, and easier mixing of even the thickest substances.

Available in beautiful mix 'n match colored handles . . . Turquoise, Pink, Black and Yellow . . . to match Flint "1900" cutlery and kitchen tools.

Handle Color	Stock No.	Factory Shpg. Ctn. Ea.	Shell Pack Ea.	Wt. Lbs. Ea.	Price
Yellow	676Y	12	1	1⅜	
Pink	676X	12	1	1⅜	
Turquoise	676T	12	1	1⅜	
Black	676	12	1	1⅜	

All Flint "Best" egg beaters are individually gift boxed

The NEW RHYTHM Beaters

Solid die cast gear wheel, balanced for faster, easier operation.

Long protective skirt keeps nylon gears from damage, makes cleaning effortless.

Stainless support band provides rugged staking, adds sturdiness and durability.

Ekco/Flint Rhythm Beaters from an Ekco Products catalog. This was Ekco's top-of-the-line beater in 1957, the new wavy design blades, "made their best even better!"

Ekco Egg Beaters, Flint Rhythm Beaters, lightly used in turquoise or yellow.
$18-$25

Flint Beaters, lightly used with standard blades in pink.
$22–$25

Ekco/Flint Knives ad from 1947. Ekco got into the cutlery business with the 1934 acquisition of the Geneva Cutlery Co. A later acquisition added laminated "Pakkawood" handles to the line.

Ekco/Flint Carving Set, four pieces, stainless steel with hardwood holder, boxed, 1940s-1950s.
$25-$35

When found, vintage cutlery sets usually are an excellent value. They are fun to collect, because numerous versions have been produced.

Ekco/Flint Steakster Set, six pieces, stainless steel with rosewood handles and hardwood holder. Boxed 1940s-1950s.
$18-$25

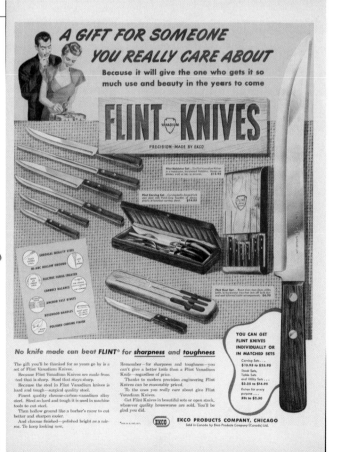

A GIFT FOR SOMEONE YOU REALLY CARE ABOUT
Because it will give the one who gets it so much use and beauty in the years to come

FLINT VANADIUM KNIVES
PRECISION · MADE BY EKCO

No knife made can beat **FLINT**® for **sharpness** and **toughness**

EKCO PRODUCTS COMPANY, CHICAGO

Ekco "1400" Kitchen Tool Set, eight pieces in red, economy set in nickel-plated steel, boxed, unused, 1950s.

$125-$150

Assorted pieces.

$15-$18 each

Ekco "2600" Kitchen Tool Set, eight pieces in turquoise, better quality set in chrome-plated steel, boxed, unused, 1950s.

$110-$125

Assorted pieces in natural with red finish.

$15-$18 each

Ekco "2600" Kitchen Tool Set, eight pieces in pink and black, chrome-plated steel, boxed, unused, 1950s.

$125-$150

Ekco "2600" Kitchen Tool Set, eight pieces in natural and black, chrome-plated steel, boxed, unused, 1950s.

$85–$100

Ekco "1900" Kitchen Tool Set, seven pieces in black, deluxe stainless steel, boxed, unused 1950s.

$75-$95

Add $30-$50 for sets in pink, yellow, or turquoise.

Ekco Kitchen Tool Set, five pieces in red and white, boxed, 1950s.

$28-$35

This set is missing a piece, reducing its value by about 25 percent.

Ekco Kitchen Tool Set, "Shower of gadgets," in white with speckled gold wood handles, boxed, early 1960s.

$50-$75

Individual pieces.

$7-$8

Ekco Kitchen Tool Set, seven pieces, "Spice Garden," with decorated plastic handles, boxed, late 1970s.

$30-$35

Ekcoline Kitchen Tools ad from the late 1940s.
$5-$7

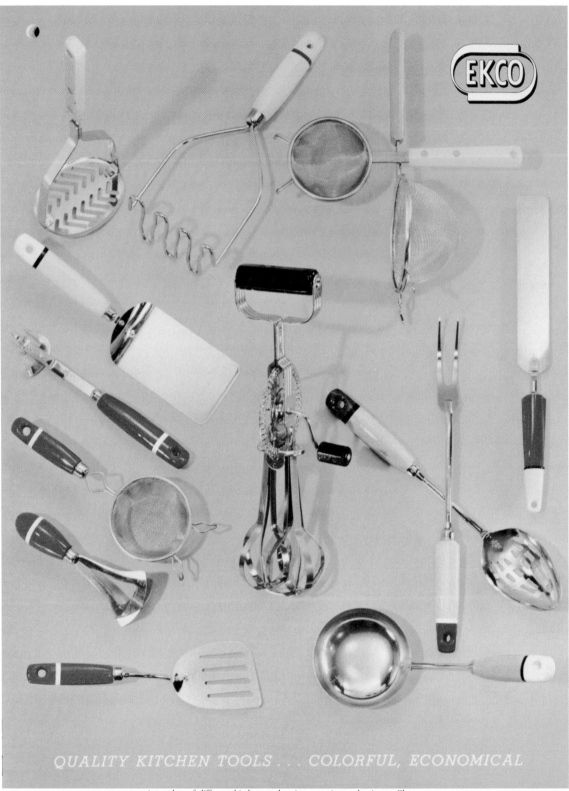

QUALITY KITCHEN TOOLS . . . COLORFUL, ECONOMICAL

A number of different kitchen tool series were in production at Ekco in the 1950s. The assortment shown is from Ekco's 1957 catalog.

Sets

Mint condition

Lightly used

$75–$150

$40-$50

Individual Pieces

Mint condition

Lightly used

$15-$18

$7-$10

Ekco 1957 70th anniversary full line catalog

$45-$65

Ekco Steak Knife Set, six pieces, stainless steel with laminated "Pakkawood" handles, boxed, 1950s.

$15-$18

Ekco Tableware, Baguette stainless steel, six place settings, boxed, 1961.

$30-$35

Ekco/Mary Ann Rolling Pin, boxed, unused, 1940s.

$35-$40

Meat Tenderizer, lightly used, 1940s.

$12-$15

These products have distinct wavy wood handles and are unmarked.

Potato Masher, boxed, unused, 1940s.

$28-$35

Ekco/Miracle Ice Cream Scoop, stainless steel with plastic handle, 1950s.

$18-$22

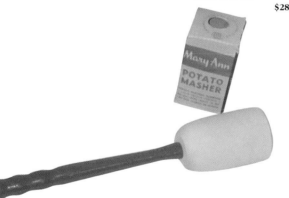

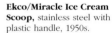

Ekco Shoe Stretchers, 1950s. Although this product may seem incompatible with Ekco's kitchen items, closer examination reveals a similarity in materials and manufacturing processes.

$5-$8 pair

Ekco/Miracle Cup Rack, "pull out–push in with a touch of the finger," with insert card, 1950s.

$10-$12

Ekco Pants Creasers, with label, 1950s.

$15-$18

Ekco Pressure Cooker ad from *Better Homes and Gardens*, February, 1947.

$2-$3

Users were cautioned to practice opening the tricky top mechanism a few times before removing the label.

Ekco Pressure Cooker, with serving cover and recipe booklet, 1940s.

$18-$25

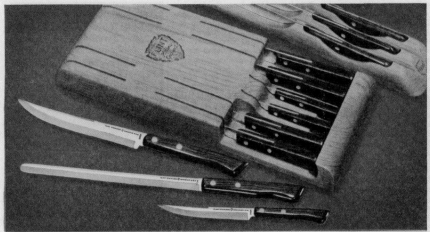

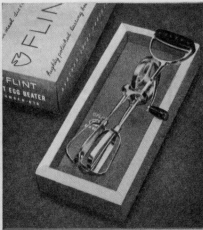

Perfect for the Donovans ... **OR FOR YOU!**

... Ekco Flint Cutlery, America's most wanted quality knives. Sparkling blades of "Ekco-Temp" stainless steel, fortified with toughening vanadium. "Hi-Arc" hollow ground blades—won't need sharpening for years. Glowing lifetime handles of genuine imported rosewood

—fit the hand perfectly. Featured is the famous hardwood hang-up Holdster Set of six essential knives—from 3″ paring knife to 9½″ ham slicer. Packed in stunning gift box, ready for Christmas wrapping. Single knives individually gift boxed, from 79c. Sets from $3.50. Set featured $16.95.

For those "Good Mixers", the Udells ... **OR FOR YOU!**

...the Ekco "Best" Food Mixer ... the world's fastest and built to last a lifetime. Has bakelite comfort-grip handle and stainless steel blades. "Nylon" geared to last longer, run smoother, give mixer results by hand, and won't tire the arm. Won't wobble or splash in any size bowl. In handsome gift box. $4.95.

Grand gift for the Wilsons ... **OR FOR YOU!**

...Ekcoware Copper Bottom Utensils, matchless for beauty. Heavy stainless steel for cleaning ease ... thick copper bottoms for cooking speed. Stay-cool handles that hang up. Domed, tight-fitting, self-basting lids. Ekcoware's a practical gift that will be prized for years. Single pieces from $3.40.

Beautiful, Practical Gifts...AND A JOY TO USE!

For wife, mother, home-maker friend or you ... nothing can match the year 'round beauty and usefulness of these outstanding kitchen helps. They sparkle like gems and make cooking and serving far easier. Even the gift packaging is stunning—in perfect taste. And every one bears the fine name Ekco, hallmark of America's most wanted housewares. At better stores everywhere.

You give... and get the best when it's labeled **EKCO**

THE BIGGEST NAME IN HOUSEWARES
EKCO PRODUCTS COMPANY, CHICAGO 39, ILLINOIS

A welcome gift for the Crawfords ... **OR FOR YOU!**

the new Ekconomic Low Pressure Cooker. Cooks meats, fowl, fish to oven goodness—*at pressure pan speed.* Secret is the new Ekco-Lo 3¾ lb. control (also has 15 lb. and 10 lb. control, for canning, stews, soups). Simple, safe—the only pressure cooker to win National Home Safety Award. 5-qt. size—$14.95 (including big recipe book).

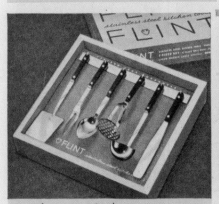

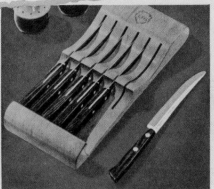

Aunt Gert will love this ... **SO WILL YOU!**

... Ekco Flint Kitchen Tools ... so gracefully designed, so precisely balanced, they make kitchen-chores far easier. Guaranteed 15 years. Stainless steel surfaces are taperground like fine cutlery—tarnish proof. Easy-grip hang-up handles. 7-piece set at $12.95 shown. Single pieces from $1.75. Sets from $6.95.

"Super" for the Adams family ... **OR FOR YOU!**

... the superb Ekco Flint "Steakster Set." Six gleaming steak-and-chop knives in a hardwood block. Blades of "Ekco-Temp" stainless steel fortified with vanadium. Keen cutting serrated edges never need sharpening! Rich, imported rosewood handles fit the hand perfectly. A wonderful gift, and only $9.95.

A beauty for the Paytons ... **OR FOR YOU!**

... gay, colorful Ekcoline Kitchen Tools. Graceful design ... stainless steel working surfaces with plastic handles in red or yellow. Hanging on a stainless steel rack, Ekcoline Tools bring beauty and efficiency to any kitchen. Set shown, 7 essential tools and wall rack, in gift box, $7.50. Single pieces from 69c.

Ekco ad showing gift selections from the early 1950s.
$5-$7

Ekco Products Co. ❖ 37

Chapter 3

The Gadget Department at Ekco

A number of companies embraced the field of gadgets and actively pursued multiple product entries in this category. These included Ekco Products Co., Foley Manufacturing co., The Washburn Co.(Androck), The Vaughan Manufacturing Co., and others.

Ekco Products Co., was a leading player and could be described as the king of the gadget field in the 1950s. Along with carded and loose items, Ekco created large merchandising racks and shelving units to prominently display their line. Pictured are typical gadget rack and shelf units from the 1950s era, fully stocked with consumer-tempting entries.

By the mid-1950s a company pamphlet was proclaiming, "Its fun to play with the Ekco gadgets of today." The fun seems not to have abated as vintage gadgets of all sorts by Ekco find acceptance with collectors for display or use.

Ekco Gadget and Housewares Center, from a 1957 Ekco catalog.

Ekco Tomato Slicer, marked Tomado made in Holland, with card sleeve, 1950s.

$15-$18

Ekco/Miracle Tomato Slicer, with card sleeve, 1950s.

$15-$18

Ekco Tomato Slicer, one cut makes eleven perfect slices, with card sleeve, 1959.

$15-$18

Ekco Juice Strainer, metal, "get all the goodness of fresh fruit," on card, 1959.

$12-$15

Ekco Flavor-It, aluminum, "For juicing garlic, onion, mint. So easy just squeeze," on card, 1950s.

$20-$22

Ekco Garlic Press, "One squeeze adds zest to any foods," on card, 1959.

$20-$22

Ekco/Miracle French Fry Cutter, metal with stainless steel blade and wooden handle, "Cuts 25 pieces with one stroke," boxed, 1950s.

$22-$25

Ekco Measuring Cup Set, aluminum, four pieces, "Accurate sizes," in package, 1950s.

$20-$22

Page from a 1950s Ekco advertising pamphlet.
$10-$12

Kitchen Gadgets from Ekco's 1957 full line catalog.

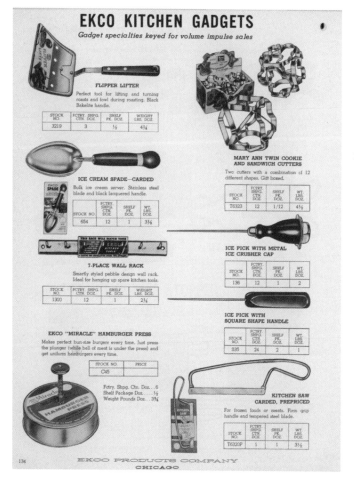

Ekco Miracle Gem Strainer, metal pop-out design with decorated side walls, 1950s.

$8-$12

Ekco/Miracle Can Opener, display box, 1950s.

$15-$18

Originally from Wark's hardware store in Valparaiso, IN, box came filled with can openers for individual purchase, openers.

$3-$5 each

Ekco Peeler, metal, "Nee action with floating blade, Safe, Simple, Fast," on card, 1950s.

$15-$18

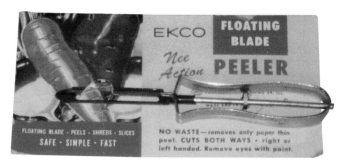

Ekco/Eterna Utility Tongs, "For everything hot and cold," with sleeve, 1950s.

$12-$15

Ekco Rolling Pin, wood ball bearing, natural and black handles, with label, 1958.

$28-$35

Ekco Hand Mixer, natural and black handle, 1950s.

$15-$18

Ekco Kitchamajig Stirrer and Strainer, natural and black handle, 1950s.

$15-$18

Ekco Flipper/Lifter, "Flips omelets, pancakes, etc.," natural and black handle, with label, 1950s.

$18-$20

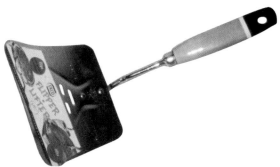

Ekco Peeler, metal, "Nee action with floating blade and green bean slicer, Shreds, Peels, Slices," on card, 1950s.

$15-$18

Ekco Peeler, metal, with bean slicer, "Floating action," on card, 1961.

$10-$12

Ekco Presto-Whip, metal, "Whips, Blends, Mixes, with double action coiled bottom," with card sleeve, 1960.

$12-$15

Ekco Presto-Whip, metal, "Beats, Mixes, Whips," with card sleeve, 1950s.

$12-$15

Ekco Tea Strainer, metal, "A pleasure to use, Strains better, Cleans easier, on card, 1950s.

$15-$18

Ekco/Autoyre Soap Saver, keeps soap dry and clean, on card, 1958.

$10-$12

Ekco Baller, Fruit and Potato, metal with black and natural wood center section, "Makes large or small balls for that party time touch," on card, 1958.

$18-$20

Ekco Baller, 2-in-1 fruit and potato, metal with red wood center section, for parties and everyday delicacies, on card, 1958.

$18-$20

Ekco Pastry Crimper and Trimmer, metal and plastic with black and natural wood center section, "Edges, trims, and seals," on card, 1959.

$18-$20

Ekco Pie Crimper, "gift them with a gadget," metal and plastic with red wood center section, on card, 1950s. Top portion tears off for use as a combination gift and card. Ekco/Canada Ltd.

$18-$20

Ekco/Bull-Dog Bottle Stoppers, "Keeps fizz in," on card, 1960s.

$10-$12

Ekco/Miracle Cap Lifter, metal, vacuum jar and bottle, on card, 1950s.

$12-$15

Ekco Lid Flipper, vacuum jar, and bottle, on card, 1950s.

$10-$12

Ekco Pair-O-Gadgets, two handy openers, metal, on card, 1957.

$12-$15

Ekco Wall Can Opener, metal, with tool steel cutter, on card, 1959.

$18-$22

Ekco Foilware, ten 4" reusable aluminum pie plates, in package, 1950s.

$8-$10

Ekco Jar Wrench, metal, on card, 1970s.

$5-$8

Ekco Cheese-Slicer Server, metal with plastic handle, on card, 1970s.

$5-$8

Ekco Peeler, metal, "Nee action with slip-proof handle," on card, 1970s.

$5-$8

Ekco Can Piercer, metal, "Leaves no jagged edges," on card, 1960s.

$6-$8

Ekco Can Opener, metal with coated plastic handles, "Easy action," on card 1960s.

$8-$10

Ekco Baking Rack, aluminum, "Four in one," on card, 1970s.

$5-$8

Ekco Knife Sharpener, metal with wood handle, on card, 1960s.

$8-$10

Ekco Pizza Cutter, metal with black plastic handle, on card, 1970s.

$5-$8

Chapter 4

Foley Manufacturing Company

The Foley Manufacturing Co. of Minneapolis, MN was founded by Walter Ringer, Sr., in 1926. Their first kitchenware product was a food mill licensed from a foreign patent in 1933. It gained acceptance during the Depression as a thrifty food preparation and canning device. The food mill continued to be a successful product for many years and is still in production today. Other early Foley products were a food chopper and a blending fork.

During World War II, kitchenware production at Foley was temporarily halted so that efforts could be concentrated on producing mess kits and other necessities for the war effort. When postwar production resumed, Foley expanded its operations by acquiring the Meets-a-Need Co. and their Sift-Chine flour sifter, and started making sifters under the Foley name.

Throughout the 1950s & 1960s, Foley continued to introduce new products including handheld juicers, shredders, measuring tools, etc., that expanded their kitchenware line. In the 1960s, a number of items were made for Foley in Japan by other companies. During 1984, the Foley kitchen tools, gadgets, and cookware became part of the Newell companies, and production continued as the Foley-Martens Co. Products are currently manufactured at a plant in Kingsford, MI.

Today, vintage Foley products offer interest to a wide range of kitchen collectors. Their early products with wood handles and simple mechanisms appeal to collectors of Depression-era kitchenware. Sifters, shredders, and other products from the 1950s and later appeal to collectors interested in items of more recent vintage. Because many Foley products were such useful kitchen necessities, finding them in mint condition with labeling intact is very difficult.

Foley Rolling Pin, wood, precision ball bearing, with label 1950s.

$25-$28

Foley Three-screen Sifter, aluminum, "Always sift to bake your best with any flour," with label 1950s-1960s.

$15-$20

Foley Pastry Cloth, with rolling pin cover, "Rolls flakier pastry faster!," in package, 1950s.

$12-$15

Foley Cookie Dropper, metal, "Easiest way to make cookies!," on card, 1950s, either version.

$15-$18

---

by Foley

Guaranteed by Good Housekeeping
REPLACEMENT OR A REFUND OF MONEY IF NOT AS ADVERTISED THEREIN

FOOD MILL

Household Size

HOUSEHOLD SIZE—A potato ricer, vegetable masher, fruit strainer. Wizard-like, it slashes minutes from meal making! For family foods, for baby foods, for canning. 24-gauge steel, tin-coated. Capacity 2 quarts. Price **$1⁸⁹**

BABY SIZE—Designed especially for straining individual food portions for baby or adult smooth diets. 24-gauge steel, tin-coated. Capacity 1 qt. Price **$1⁶⁹**

MASTER SIZE—For quantity home canning. Strains bushel tomatoes into juice in 12 minutes. Cans apple butter or sauce in minimum time. For quantity food preparation in hotels, restaurants, hospitals, schools, institutions. 20-gauge steel, tin-coated. Capacity 5 qts. Price **$5⁹⁵**

FOLEY SIFTER

5-CUP SIZE

"Big Sister". Screen removable for easy cleaning. Single screen meets all sifting requirements. Aluminum, quick spring action steel handle. Price **$1³⁹**

SIFTER

2-CUP SIZE

"Jr. Miss". Measures as it sifts directly into cup. Coned bottom, single screen. Aluminum. Price . . **69¢**

SIFTER

FOLEY BLENDER

Cuts, creams, beats, mixes! Prongs slanted for quick pastry-blending, cake-mixing, salad-tossing, gravy-making. Nestles in mixing bowl. Stainless steel. Price . . . . **39¢**

BLENDER

FOLEY CHOPPER

Skips through every chopping chore! Shreds, chops cabbage. Cubes steak. Chops onions, parsley, pickles. Tenderizes meats. 3 stainless blades with spring action. Price . . . . **79¢**

CHOPPER

Sold on money back-guarantee

FOLEY MANUFACTURING CO., MINNEAPOLIS 18, MINN.

NATIONALLY ADVERTISED

161

Foley ad from *House Furnishing Review*, July 10, 1948.

Foley Juicer, aluminum, "Fits over cup, strains as it juices," on card, 1950s, either version.

$15-$18

Foley Shredder, stainless steel, on card, 1950s.

$15-$18

Foley Hand Grater, stainless steel, on card, 1950s.

$12-$15

Foley Tongs, metal, "For lifting, turning, serving," on card, 1950s.

$12-$15

Foley Baster, glass with rubber bulb, "For skimming excess fats, gravies, soups," with sleeve, 1950s.

$15-$18

Foley Strainer, metal with wood handle, 1950s.

$10-$12

Foley Three-screen Sifter, metal, sifts into cup, with label, 1940s-1950s.

$15-$18

Foley Chopper, triple knife blade action with wood handle, "For cabbages, vegetables, fruits, nuts, etc.," boxed, 1940s-1950s.

$18-$22

Foley Food Mill, made in three sizes, metal with wood handle, "Mashes, Rices, Strains all cooked foods," with label, 1940s-1950s.

$30-$35

Foley Measuring Spoons, aluminum, "Guaranteed accurate," on card, 1960s.

$15-$18

Foley Coffee Measure, aluminum, on card, 1960s.

$12-$15

Foley Knife Sharpener, plastic, "Newest principle in sharpening," boxed, 1950s.

$15-$18

Collier's Magazine, February 14, 1953. The small boy in the cowboy hat is shown recklessly swinging from a cart during a 1950s shopping trip, maybe this scene helped inspire the term shopping spree.

$8-$10

Chapter 5

The Washburn Company (Androck)

Charles Washburn founded the company in 1880 and moved it from Boston to Worcester, MA. He incorporated it as the Wire Goods Company in 1882. A Chicago-based division, the Wire Hardware Company, was started in 1911 and merged with the Andrews Wire and Iron Works of Rockford, IL in 1917. These companies and another manufacturer became the Washburn Company in 1922. Its operations were consolidated at Rockford, IL, and Worcester, MA, in 1929.

The 1920s saw the Washburn company adopt colorful painted wood handles on their Androck kitchenware. In 1934, Androck utensils were introduced featuring tear-shaped handles in red, yellow, and green Catalin plastic. This line was successful into the 1940s. Wartime production replaced kitchenware at the Washburn Co. for a time during the 1940s and after production resumed, a two-color styrene plastic handle utensil line was introduced that was lighter in weight and less expensive than the earlier Catalin utensils. Over the years, the Washburn company put the Androck name on additional kitchenware items including onion and nut choppers and gadgets.

The Androck line of flour sifters was continuously improved and expanded. In the 1940s & 1950s, Androck's designs on sifters culminated in a series of colorful "pantry pattern" three screen models including a mom and kids in the kitchen design which has grown in popularity with collectors.

In 1967, Roblin Steel Corp. of Buffalo, NY, acquired the Washburn Co. They closed the Rockford plant and consolidated production at Worcester, MA, plant in 1973. The Canadian branch of the company became a separate entity and the Worcester plant was dissolved in 1975. Various equipment and tooling went to several companies, and the Androck name continued appearing on products from multiple sources after 1975.

Today, Androck's plastic-handled utensils from the 1930s and 1940s are sought after by collectors who treasure examples showing minimal wear or discoloration. Androck flour sifters from the 1940s and 1950s with their colorful printed designs are also collector favorites. Interest continues to grow for later Androck gadgets, utensils, and other kitchenware.

Woman's Day, January 1956. This neatly dressed 1950s family is showing off their "dinner for 4 for $1."

$6-$8

Androck Utensils, Bakelite (Catalin) plastic 1930s-1940s, available in red, yellow, and green. Examples without discoloration or other flaws bring the highest prices. Eggbeater

$25-$28

Potato masher, ladle, pastry blender, fork, spreader

$18-$22 each

Androck Kitchen Tools Gift Set, stainless steel with yellow and green handles, boxed, unused 1940s-1950s.

$100-$125

Androck Eggbeaters, marked "Another Androck Product," yellow and green plastic handle 1940s–1950s.

$22-$25

Androck Eggbeaters, Red wooden handle, 1940s-1950s.

$18-$22

Androck "Tearless" Onion Chopper, "Fumes can't get out–ends tearful task," stainless steel blades with wooden handle, unused, with label, 1950s.

$35-$40

Androck Nut Chopper, unused, with label, 1940s-1950s.

$35-$40

Androck Onion Chopper, 1950s-1960s.

$12-$15

Androck Nut Chopper, 1950s-1960s.

$12-$15

Androck Nut Chopper, with label, 1960s.

$18-$20

Androck Sugar Meter, with label, 1960s.

$18-$20

Androck Mellon Baller, "For making salads and fruit cup," metal, with natural and red wood center section, on card, 1950s.

$15-$18

Androck Nut Meat Chopper, "The kitchen's handiest helper," boxed, 1930s-1940s.

$25-$28

Androck Cake Mixer and Egg Whip, with insert card, 1950s, either version.

$10-$12

NEW

5000 LINE OF
Stainless Steel
KITCHEN TOOLS

Bright Polished Finish. Red and ivory plastic handles.

ANDROCK 5 sizes of Food Strainers in matching design.

© 1951

THE WASHBURN COMPANY
WORCESTER, MASS. • ROCKFORD, ILL.

Androck ad from *House Furnishing Review*, 1951.

Chapter 6

Flour Sifters

Flour sifters are a handy kitchen accessory for aerating flour and promoting even, lump-free baking. Sifters having a single screen with a simple rotating mechanism were developed in the 1920s, and later improvements, such as multiple screens and trigger-spring action, allowed better sifting and one-hand operation. Colorful printed metal designs from the 1940s and 1950s added appeal when new, and are still popular with collectors today. With flour sifters the variety of designs produced over the years practically assures a match to anyone's kitchen decor or interest level.

Androck Flour Sifter
three screens, "Hand-I-Sift," red and white "Pantry Pattern" design with bakery items, 1950s.

$25-$30

Androck Flour Sifter,
three screens, yellow with flower design and wood handle, 1940s.

$22-$25

Now—with covers!

ANDROCK 3-SCREEN
Flour Sifter

Easier to fill . . . cleaner to store . . . stops leakage

Androck Sifter No. 773 has *everything*—3 screens . . . one-hand operation . . . new metal slip-on covers top and *bottom.* Easier to fill. No leaking. Shelf stays clean. Wonderful gift. Try its easy action at department, chain, hardware stores, super markets. $1.98.

THE WASHBURN COMPANY, Worcester, Mass., Rockford, Ill.

Androck three-screen flour sifter ad from *Good Housekeeping*, June 1954.

ANDROCK
timesaving
FLOUR SIFTER

SIFT FLOUR JUST
ONCE THROUGH 3 SCREENS

One hand does it! Get fluffier, lighter flour! 4-cup size.

Pantry Patterns $1.89
Chrome sifter $2.79

QUALITY PRODUCTS SINCE 1880
THE WASHBURN COMPANY
Worcester, Massachusetts   **Rockford, Illinois**

Androck "Pantry Patterns" Flour Sifter ad from *Good Housekeeping*, November 1955.

"Sift-Chine" Flour Sifter, three screens with wooden handle and knob, cream with orange bands, 1930s-1940s, Meets–A-Need Co., Seattle WA.

$18-$20

Foley Mfg. Co. acquired the Meets-A-Need Co., and "Sift-Chine" in the 1940s.

"Sift-Chine" Flour Sifter, "guaranteed satisfactory," chrome with yellow bands, 1940s.

$18-$20

Androck Flour Sifter, three screens, floral design with wooden handle and knob, 1940s.

$22-$25

Androck Flour Sifter, three screens, "Hand-I-Sift," wheat stalk and bakery items design, 1950s.

$25-$30

Androck Flour Sifter, three screens, "Hand-I-Sift," mom and kids in the kitchen design, 1950s.

$35-$65

Androck Flour Sifter, three screens with geometric pattern, 1950s-1960s.

$15-$18

Androck Flour Sifter, three screen with yellow and red abstract design, 1960s.

$15-$18

Androck Flour Sifter, three screen in chrome, with label, 1950s.

$18-$20

Foley Flour Sifter, three screen in copper, marked Foley "Sift-Chine," with label, 1950s.

$25-$30

Triple Screen Flour Sifter, three screen capacity, with label, 1960s, Aluminum Housewares Co., St. Louis, MO.

$15-$18

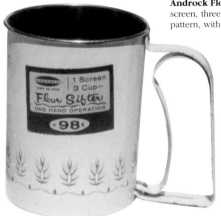

Androck Flour Sifter, one screen, three cup, floral pattern, with label, 1950s.

$15-$18

Foley Flour Sifter, screen, with label, 1960s-1970s.

$8-$10

Foley Flour Sifter, five cup, aluminum, comes apart to wash, with label, 1950s.

$28-$35

Flour Sifter, triple screen, copper-toned, aluminum and pink handle, with label, 1950s-1960s Aluminum Housewares Co., St. Louis, MO.

$28-$35

Flour Sifter, crank-type mechanism, strawberry design with wooden handle, unmarked, 1950s.

$18-$20

Flour Sifter, crank-type mechanism, daisy design with wooden handle, unmarked, 1950s.

$18-$20

Flour Sifter, crank-type mechanism, apple design with wooden handle, 1950s.

$20-$25

Bromwell Products, div. of Leigh, Inc., Michigan City, IN. This kitchen gadget was made in my hometown.

Flour Sifter, three screen, with label, 1960s, Bromwell Products.

$8-$10

Reversible Multi-Sift, two-chamber design in red and clear plastic, "Sift, click, resift, as many times as needed," boxed. 1950s, Na-Mac Products Corp., Los Angeles, CA.

$28-$35

Flour Sifter, five cup, styrene plastic with metal screen and mechanism, flower design, and graduations, 1950s, Popeil Bros., Chicago, IL.

$18-$22

Flour Sifter, two cup, styrene plastic with metal screen and mechanism, tea rose design, 1950s. no label

$15-$18

with label

$18-$22

Chapter 7

Beaters, Mixers, Whippers

B eaters are used to whip cream, eggs, batter, etc. and generally fall into three broad categories: fixed, mechanical, or rotary. Fixed beaters are guided by hand motion and include simple wire and coiled wire designs. Mechanical beaters involve pushing up and down on the top to create a revolving motion. Rotary beaters involve a geared wheel and crank mechanism where rotating blades create the mixing action. Rotary whippers usually have a faster motion that adds additional aeration to the mixture. Beater design has evolved from early primitive examples to modern-era stainless steel and plastic versions. With the number and variety of beaters made over the years, collectors are assured of finding a wide range of items to interest them.

Eggbeater, natural and red wooden handle, "Another Androck Product," 1940s-1950s.

$22-$25

Eggbeater, stainless steel, cast-metal gear, brown wooden handle, Maid of Honor, 1950s.

$15-$18

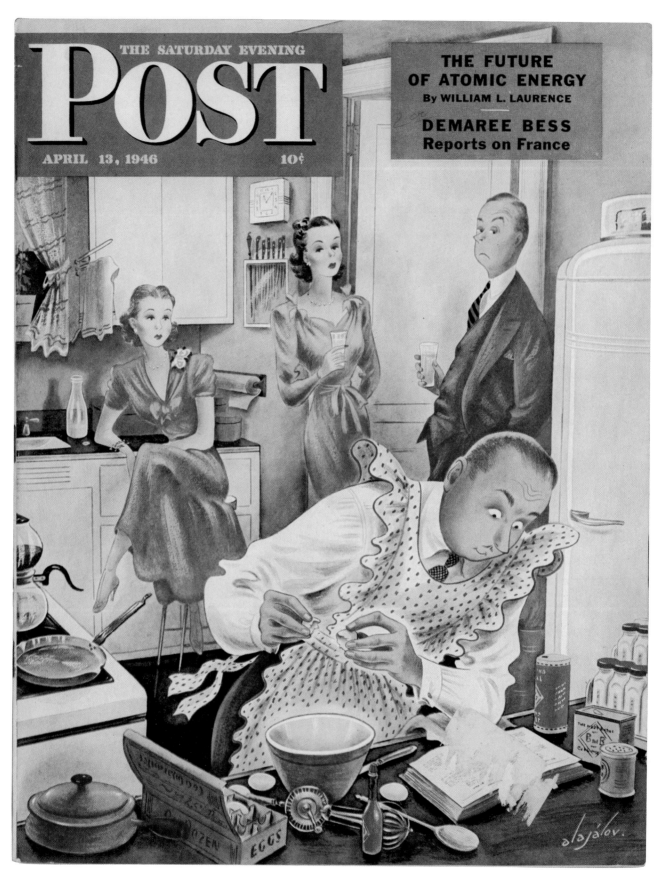

Saturday Evening Post, April 13, 1946, cover illustration by Constantin
Alajalov. It looks like the gentleman shown fell behind in his party
preparations and some guests have joined him in the kitchen, but they
don't seem to be having a good time.

$8-$10

Eggbeater, A&J high speed, green wooden handle, Ekco Products Co., 1940s-1950s.

$15-$18

Eggbeater, metal with adjustable top handle, 1940s-1950s, Dazey Mfg. Co., St. Louis, MO.

$20-$25

Eggbeater, with green Bakelite side handle, 1940s, Worlbeater, Los Angeles, CA.

$30-$35

Eggbeater, with yellow Bakelite handle, 1940s A&J High Speed, Ekco Products Co.

$20-$22

Eggbeater, cast-metal components, black plastic handle, 1950s, Rival Mfg. Co., St. Louis, MO.

$20-$22

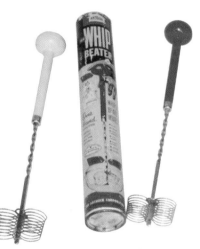

Artbeck Whip Beater, with plastic knob, "Whips, beats, mixes, one hand operation," with tube carton, 1954, Arthur Beck Co., Chicago, IL.

$15-$18

Whip Beater, red and white plastic knob, unmarked, 1950s.

$10-$12

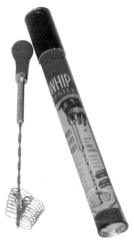

Artbeck Whip Beater, wooden knob, with tube carton, 1948.

$20-$22

Mix Matic Food Mixer, "Mixes, beats, whips, blends," boxed, 1950s-1960s, E-Z-Por Corp., Chicago, IL.

$22-$25

Speed Mixer, stainless steel and plastic with enclosed housing, "Designed for cleanliness," boxed, 1950s, Maynard Mfg. Co., Glendale, CA.

$35-$40

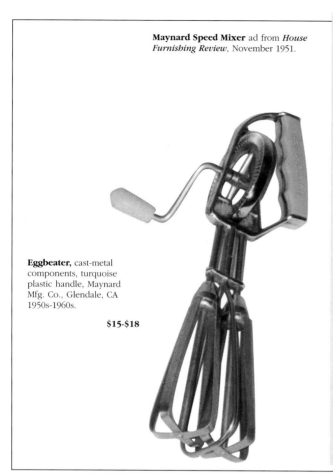

Maynard Speed Mixer ad from *House Furnishing Review*, November 1951.

Eggbeater, cast-metal components, turquoise plastic handle, Maynard Mfg. Co., Glendale, CA 1950s-1960s.

$15-$18

Quality Mixers at Low Cost

← Perfect position for ease of operation

← Gay Tenite Colors

REPLACEMENT OR REFUND OF MONEY
Guaranteed by
Good Housekeeping
IF NOT AS ADVERTISED THEREIN

← Designed for Cleanliness

← Stainless Steel

← Deep-set, Bell Bottom Blades Sit Low in Liquids

SPEEDY MIXER

Fastest available and featuring the Maynard "Sanitary Safety Seal."

MAYNARD MODEL #77

May we send you our catalog sheet?

MAYNARD
MANUFACTURING COMPANY
1444 East Colorado Blvd.,
Glendale 5, Cal.

Blue whirl
BALL BEARING BEATER

8 Reasons why it's the Best Buy in Beaters

1 PLASTIC HANDLE AND KNOB.
Easy to grasp. Will not crack.
2 BALL BEARING DRIVE.
The crank spins easily.
3 NEW LARGE GEAR WHEEL.
For faster, smoother action.
4 PROTECTIVE GEAR SHIELD.
Protection from moving parts.
5 SLEEVE TYPE PINIONS.
Prevent jamming of floats.
6 EASY TO CLEAN.
Stainless steel floats and wings.
7 STATIONARY WINGS.
Provide efficient action.
8 FLATTENED CENTER WIRE.
For close contact to bowl.

T&S
TORRINGTON

Blue Whirl is furnished in two popular sizes, the medium household size No. 55 and the large hotel or restaurant size No. 60. Both are packed individually and supplied with green, red or yellow plastic handles. For free literature and prices write . . .

The Turner & Seymour Mfg. Co.,
TORRINGTON, CONNECTICUT

Blue Whirl Beater ad from *House Furnishing Review*, May 1951.

Blue Whirl Eggbeater, stainless-steel blades, plastic handle, 1950s, The Turner & Seymour Co., Torrington, NC.

$18-$22

Dazey Mix-er-ator, with graduations and mixing directions, 1950s, Dazey Corp., St. Louis, MO.

$20-$25

Whixit Mixer, with graduations, 1950s, Taylor Churn Co, St. Louis, MO.

$18-$20

Speed-E-Whipper, "Its amazing, beats, blends, whips, mixes, and many other uses you yourself will discover," yellow with embossed glass, 1950s.

$18-$22

Red with printed glass, boxed, 1950s.

$25-$28

Includes special mail-in offer from Golden Guernsey Dairy. L B Sales Co., Los Angeles, CA.

Jiffywhip Whipper, "Whips any quantity eggs, batters, cream," boxed, 1940s-1950s, R Krasberg & Sons, Chicago, IL.

$25-$28

Minit Cream Whip, "The Wonder," green wooden handle, boxed, 1930s-1940s, D-M Mfg. Co., Detroit, MI.

$35-$40

Duplex Whipper, metal with green wood handle, "Double action for cream, eggs, and dressings," boxed, 1930s-1940s.

$40-$45

A&J/Ekco Whippit, "Whips cream in an instant," boxed, 1930s-1940s, Ekco Products Co., Chicago, IL.

$35-$40

Whippit, cream and egg whip, "They all say whip it with whippit–more than 500,000 users," marbled green wooden handle, boxed, 1930s-1940s, Indestro Mfg. Co., Chicago, IL.

$40-$45

Chapter 8

Cake and Mold Pans

Vintage cake and mold pans come in a variety of shapes and sizes. Many pans were created to help celebrate holidays, birthdays, and other events. The pan shape sometimes helps determine the event to be celebrated such as a heart for Valentine's Day or a tree or star for Christmas. Most pans from the 1930s to 1960s originally were sold with colorful, graphically interesting labels or packaging. These materials usually provided information on product use and suggested recipes. It's not common to find a vintage pan with its original label, since use of the product usually meant removing the label. However, some labels were saved over the years for their recipes. Expect to pay a 35% or higher premium for a vintage pan still retaining its original label. Cake and mold pans having a figural shape or including the design of a well-known, licensed character usually have increased collector value.

Collier's, June 6, 1953 with cover illustration by Glenn Grohe. Unusual cake decorating scene shows cowboys trying to recreate a luscious cake from a magazine ad.
$8-$10

**Kate Smith's Bake-a-Cake
Kit,** with two pans, recipe
booklets, and product
samples, boxed, 1930s.

$40-$45

Calumet tin

$18-$20

Baker's Coconut can

$15-$18

Baker's Chocolate box

$10-$15

**Ekco/Ovenex Layer Cake
Pan,** aluminum, with label,
1950s, Ekco Products Co.,
Chicago, IL.

$12-$15

**Ekco/Ecolay Layer Cake
Pan,** with label, 1950s,
Ekco Products Co.

$12-$15

Mirro Spring-Form Pan,
aluminum, "Clampless, for
Tortes, Cakes, Desserts,"
boxed, 1950s, Mirro
Aluminum, Manitowoc, WI.

$20-$25

Mirro Cake Pan,
aluminum, "Bakes all 3
perfectly, Chiffon, Sponge
Cake, and Angel Food,"
with label, 1950s, Mirro
Aluminum.

$18-$20

Mirro Layer Cake Pan,
aluminum, "Loose bottom
for easily removing cakes,"
with label, 1950s, Mirro
Aluminum.

$12-$15

**Bake King Layer Cake
Pan,** with label, 1960s,
Alcan Metallic, Lake Zurich,
IL.

$8-$12

Tier Cake Pan Set, "So
easy to make a beautiful 4-
tier cake," boxed, 1950s.

$20-$25

Saturday Evening Post, May 21, 1955 with cover illustration by Stevan Dohanos. A discouraged lass is shown in her modern kitchen losing the battle with an uncooperative cake.

Mirro 4-Tier Cake Pan Set, aluminum, "For parties, holidays, every gala occasion," boxed, 1950s, Mirro Aluminum, Manitowoc, WI.

$18-$22

4-Piece Tier Cake Set, boxed 1950s, Bake King, Chicago Metallic Mfg. Co., Chicago, IL.

$20-$25

4-Tier Party Cake Set, aluminum, "as easy to bake as a layer cake," boxed, 1950s, Vitality Aluminum, a Mirro product, Manitowoc, WI.

$18-$22

3-Tier Cake Pan Set, "For birthdays, parties, etc.," in package, 1950s, Bake King, Chicago Metallic Mfg. Co., Chicago, IL.

$18-$20

Partycake 3-Tier Cake Pan Set, in package, 1950s, Masonware Co., div. of Fram Corp., E. Providence, RI.

$18-$20

Party Cake Pans, 3-tier set, "For your next party," boxed 1950s.

$18-$22

Rudolph the Red Nosed Reindeer Cake and Mold Pan Set, 8 pieces, copyright 1939, Robert L. May, boxed, 1950s, Bake King, Chicago Metallic Mfg. Co., Chicago, IL.

$45-$55

Lamb and Bunny Set, 10-piece aluminum, boxed, 1950s, Blue Ribbon Bakeware, Downers Grove, IL.

$25-$30

This set also appeals to collectors of Christmas and Rudolph items, boxes showing minimal wear command top prices. A later version has green lettering.

Checkered Marble Cake Pan Set, boxed, 1940s, Chicago Metallic Mfg. Co., Chicago, IL.

$22-$25

Checkered Marble Cake Pan Set, boxed, 1950s, Bake King, Chicago Metallic Mfg. Co.

$20-$22

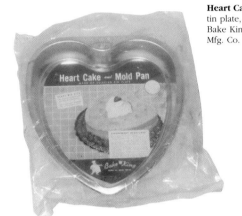

Mirro Heart Cake and Mold Set, 10 piece aluminum, "Have a heart at your next party," boxed, 1950s, Mirro Aluminum, Manitowoc, WI.

$40-$45

Heart Cake and Mold Pan, tin plate, with label, 1950s, Bake King, Chicago Metallic Mfg. Co.

$18-$20

Heart Cake and Mold Pan, with label, 1950s, Bake King, Chicago Metallic Mfg. Co.

$18-$20

Mirro Tree Cake and Mold Set, 10 piece aluminum, "Gay holiday goodies to decorate your table," boxed, 1950s, Mirro Aluminum.

$40-$45

Tree Cake Pan, tin plate, with label, 1950s, Bake King, Chicago Metallic Mfg. Co.

$18-$20

Star Mold Set, nine piece aluminum, "for distinctive appetizing," boxed, 1940s-1950s.

$22-$25

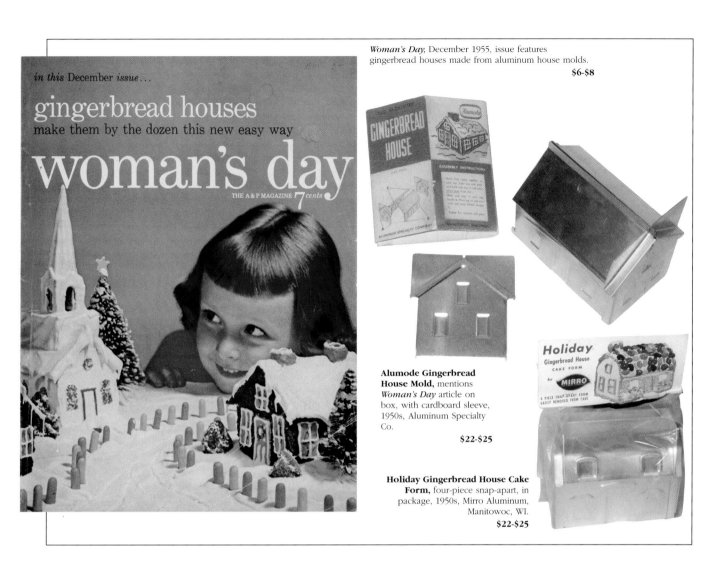

Woman's Day, December 1955, issue features gingerbread houses made from aluminum house molds.
$6-$8

Alumode Gingerbread House Mold, mentions *Woman's Day* article on box, with cardboard sleeve, 1950s, Aluminum Specialty Co.

$22-$25

Holiday Gingerbread House Cake Form, four-piece snap-apart, in package, 1950s, Mirro Aluminum, Manitowoc, WI.

$22-$25

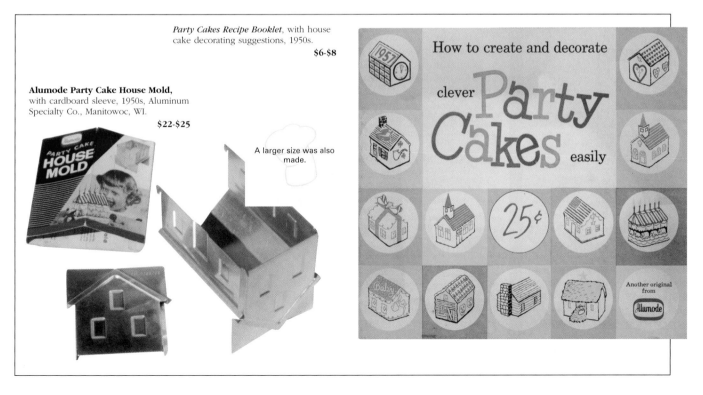

Party Cakes Recipe Booklet, with house cake decorating suggestions, 1950s.
$6-$8

Alumode Party Cake House Mold, with cardboard sleeve, 1950s, Aluminum Specialty Co., Manitowoc, WI.

$22-$25

A larger size was also made.

Easy-Out Ring Mold, "for perfect molds everytime!," boxed, 1940s, West Bend Aluminum Co., West Bend, WI.

$18-$20

Pressure Cooker and Steamer Mold, "For puddings, breads, casseroles, etc.," with label, 1950s, Bluebird brand made in Canada.

$15-$18

Wear-Ever Ring Mold Set, Melon Mold, Tart-size Pie Pans, boxed, 1950s, Aluminum Cooking Utensil Co., New Kensington, PA.

$15-$18 each

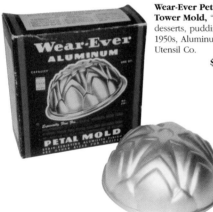

Wear-Ever Petal Mold, Tower Mold, "For salads, desserts, puddings," boxed, 1950s, Aluminum Cooking Utensil Co.

$15-$18 each

Mirro All-Purpose Molds, set of eight, "For shortcakes, salads, etc.," boxed, 1950s, Mirro Aluminum.

$18-$20

Jell-aire, six aluminum molds, "For gelatin, shells, custard pies, etc.," boxed, 1950s, Paramount Industries, New York, NY.

$15-$18

Mirro Party Mold Set, four pieces, copper-toned aluminum, with pony, duck, bunny, and squirrel molds, "For salads, desserts, etc.," in package, 1950s, Mirro Aluminum, Manitowoc, WI.

$35-$45

Mirro Mold Set, small, six pieces, copper-toned aluminum set, "For salads, gelatins, etc.," boxed, 1950s, Mirro Aluminum.

$25-$28

Mirro Mold Set, large, five pieces, copper-toned aluminum set, "For salads, gelatins, etc.," boxed, 1950s, Mirro Aluminum.

$35-$45

Miniature Copper Molds, figural molds, for desserts, salads, etc., 1950s-1960s.

$6-$8 each

Large Copper Molds, figural fish molds, for desserts, salads, etc., 1950s-1960s.

$12-$15 each

Bridge Mold Set, eight pieces, aluminum, "For molding dainty card-party desserts and salads," boxed, 1930s.

$20-$25

Eclair & Sponge Finger Moulds, six pieces, aluminum, boxed, 1950s, Thos. M Nutbrown, Ltd., Blackpool, England.

$8-$10

Mirro Jelly Molds, four-piece set, "For salads and desserts," in package, 1950s, Mirro Aluminum.

$10-$12

Four Salad Molds, heart-shaped aluminum with cookie cutter, in package, 1960s, Chiltonware, Aluminum Specialty Co., Manitowoc, WI.

$8-$10

Decorative Molds, four pieces, copper-toned aluminum, in package, 1950s-1960s, Color Craft, Indianapolis, IN.

$15-$18

Coppertone Dessert Molds, six festive patterns in heavy gold foil, in package, 1960s, E-Z Por Corp., Niles, IL.

$6-$8

Christmas Cookie Molds, heavy aluminum foil, "Bakes 24 at one time," in package, 1960s, E-Z Por Corp., Niles, IL.

$6-$8

Home Treat Ice Pop, set of four styrene plastic molds, "Make in your own kitchen," boxed, 1950s, Union Products, Leominster, MA.

$10-$12

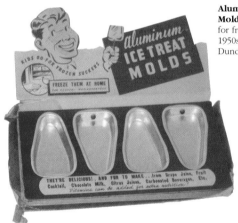

Aluminum Ice Treat Molds, set of four, "Kids go for frozen suckers," boxed, 1950s, Aldon Products Co., Duncannon, PA.

$10-$12

'Stix and Mix' Ice Treat Molds, set of four aluminum molds with sticks, boxed, 1950s, Ice Treat Inc., Newport, PA.

$10-$12

Bugs Bunny Zoo Pops, "In 4 favorite animal shapes," polyethylene plastic, copyright 1957, Warner Brothers Pictures Inc., in package.

$12-$15

Chapter 9

Cake Covers, Cake Decorations and Accessories

C akes are a special treat associated with happy events such as weddings, birthdays, and many other celebrations. Through the years, manufacturers have catered to the needs of cooks who want to give their cakes a special design or treatment by producing a wide assortment of items. Vintage accessories for decorating, trimming, cutting, and carrying cakes are increasing in popularity with collectors. In many cases, these products and their packaging illustrate the enthusiasm for the event being celebrated, making them fun to collect.

Saturday Evening Post, January 3, 1953, with cover illustration by Norman Rockwell. The portly chef is reading up on his diet while munching on a low-calorie meal, but one wonders how long he can keep it up surrounded by all those luscious cakes.

$15-$20

Better Homes

and Gardens

Serving more than 3,500,000 families
March 1952 · 25c In Canada 35c

Frostings that are lickin' good!
Pages 88 and 90

How to have a beautiful lawn this summer

Better Homes and Gardens, March 1952, small boy, who is probably more interested in sampling than mixing, tastes a frosting that is lickin' good!

$6-$8

Cake Cover, metal, yellow lid with apple design. Same pattern was used on canister sets, flour sifters, etc., 1940s-1950s.

$22-$25

Cake Cover, metal with Pennsylvania Dutch design lid, small size shown, 1940s-1950s.

$18-$22

large size

$22-$25

Cake Cover, aluminum lid with wood acorn handle and embossed side pattern, 1950s, West Bend Aluminum Co., West Bend, WI.

$18-$22

Metal cake covers in mint dent-free condition command premium prices.

Cake Cover, green-toned aluminum, "Musicake," rotating base music box plays Happy Birthday, boxed, 1950s, Heller Hostess-ware, White Plains, NY.

$35-$40

This cover also appeals to collectors of colored aluminum items.

Cake Cover, copper-tone aluminum with plastic handle and cake graphic, 1950s, West Bend Aluminum Co.

$15-$20

This commonly seen cover matches West Bend canister sets.

Cake Cover, locking copper-tone aluminum with painted base, wooden handle, and cake graphic, 1950s, Mirro Aluminum, Manitowoc, WI.

$22-$25

Cake Cover, locking copper-tone aluminum, square with wooden handle, boxed, has tag, 1950s Mirro Aluminum.

$30-$35

Cake Cover, locking styrene plastic with graphic design, 1950s-1960s, Federal Plastic Housewares, Chicago, IL.

$18-$22

Cake Cover, clear plastic, cut-glass style, 1950s-1960s.

$15-$18

Cake Cover, styrene plastic with clear "locklift" lid and embossed design, 1950s, Trans Spec Co., Cleveland, OH.

$22-$25

Cake Cover, styrene plastic with yellow "locklift" lid and embossed design, 1950s, Trans Spec Co.

$18-$22

Cake Cover, styrene plastic with clear locking lid, 1950s, Lustro-ware, Columbus Plastic Products Co, Columbus, OH.

$25-$35

Pie Cover, 'Look-n-See' locking plastic lid and aluminum bottom, 1950s, Century Aluminum.

$18-$22

Pie Cover, styrene plastic with clear locking lid and turquoise bottom, 1950s-1960s.

$18-$22

Cake Breaker, metal with yellow Bakelite handle, boxed, 1930s-1940s, C. J. Schneider Mfg. Co., Toledo, OH.

$22-$25

This example was given as a present to someone long ago, and still retains the gift card.

Hostess Cake Breaker, with brown marbled Bakelite handle, boxed, 1950s, Lagner Mfg. Co., New York, NY.

$15-$18

Cake Breaker, black or yellow Bakelite handle, 1940s.

$12-$15

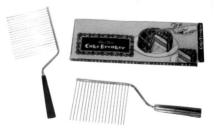

Cake Server, Kut-n-Serve, metal with plastic handles, "No fumbling, no crumbling," boxed, 1950s, Krag Steel Products, Chicago, IL.

$15-$18

Hostess Cake Caddy, metal with brown, marbled Bakelite handles, boxed, 1950s, Lagner Mfg. Co.

$15-$18

Cake Servers, orange plastic with fluted handle, 1950s, Rogers Plastic Corp., W. Warren, MA.

$2-$5

Green plastic with molded design, 1950s, marked Tico.

$10-$12

Red plastic with knob controlled gripper, hand-painted design, marked St. Petersburg, FL, 1950s.

$15-$18

Candy Cake Decorations, "Bouquet Brand" with candles. Edible cake decorations were seldom saved, and are an unusual find today, boxed, 1950s, Addis Mfg. Co., Brooklyn, NY.

$8-$12

Celebration Toast Glasses, set of 12, "For every occasion," boxed, 1950s, Maude B. May Co., Chicago, IL.

$12-$15

Cake toast glasses are almost unheard of today, largely because they were awkward to fill and only held a small amount of fluid.

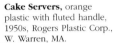

Cake Plate, ivory white with 22K gold decoration, "This new cake plate designed to cut equal pieces is wonderful!" Indentations in glass were to be used as a guide, boxed, 1950s, Anchorglass, Anchor Hocking Corp., Lancaster, OH.

$28-$30

Merry-Go-Round Birthday Candle Holders, in package, Wecolite Co., New York, NY.

$6-$8

These novel plastic candle holders attached to the side, keeping melted wax off the cake, thus giving the 1950s hostess one less thing to worry about.

Jubilee Toastettes, set of 12, plastic, "Makes every celebration happier," in package, 1950s, Shade Pulls Inc., Chicago, IL.

$8-$10

The *American Magazine*, May 1937, cover photo by Paul Hesse,
shows two kids blowing out the candles of a birthday cake.

$6-$8

Cake and Pie Knife, Spry Shortening Store Display.
$22-$25

Spry Can, 1940s.
$18-$22

Pie Knife, with yellow Bakelite handle, 1940s.
$10-$12

Aunt Jenny was Spry's spokesperson in the 1940s & 1950s and was featured in numerous ads and cookbooks.

In-Genia Layer Cake Cutter, yellow plastic and metal, "Cuts perfect layers like magic!," boxed, 1950s, Made in Germany, Overseas Housewares Co., New York, NY.
$15-$18

Shape A Cake, Santa form for cutting cake shape, boxed, 1950s, Fox Run Craftsmen, Ivyland, PA.
$18-$20

Tala Cake Marker, "For easy cake decorating," on card, 1950s, Taylor Law & Co., Ltd., Stourbridge, England.
$12-$15

Mirro Cake Knife, unbreakable, flexible plastic, on card, 1960s, Mirro Aluminum, Manitowoc, WI.
$12-$15

Cake Testers, round plastic with metal rod, on card, 1950s, M.E. Heuck Co., Cincinnati, OH.
$8-$10

Pierre Plastic Chef with metal rod, on card, 1950s, Hamblin Mfg. Co., Worcester, MA.
$12-$15

Aluminum Cake Decorator, with four tips, "Add the caterer's touch," boxed, 1940s-1950s.
$12-$15

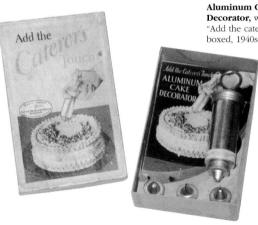

Saturday Evening Post, June 16, 1945 with cover illustration by Stevan Dohanos. This cake is obviously for a returning serviceman's wedding, and the calendar in the background showing bread being lifted gives the sense that prosperity awaits the happy couple.

$8-$10

Tala Icing Set, metal and plastic syringe with six tips, boxed, 1950s, Taylor Law & Co., Ltd., Stourbridge, England.

$18-$20

Duo-Color Cake Decorator, plastic-coated bag with nine tips, "Amazing invention makes it possible to decorate in two colors at once," boxed, 1950s, Wecolite Co., New York, NY.

$22-$25

Cake Decorator and Cookie Maker Set, transparent plastic tube with nine different tips, boxed, 1950s.

$20-$22

Cake Decorator and Flower Forming Set, orange plastic bag with pink and avocado tips, in package, 1960s.

$12-$15

Cake Decorator, aluminum with six tips, boxed, 1950s, Lorraine Metal Co., Bridgeport, CT.

$15-$18

Beautiful Cakes Decorator, aluminum with six tips, boxed, 1940s-1950s, Made in USA.

$18-$20

Ateco Decorating Set, aluminum with six tips, "there are unlimited uses of this set for the person with original ideas," boxed, 1950s, August Thomson Co., New York, NY.

$18-$20

Mirro Decorating Set, aluminum with six tips, "For cakes, cookies, pastries, etc.," boxed, 1950s, Mirro Aluminum.

$15-$18

Aluminum Cake Decorator, Happy Birthday, "for delightful, interesting cakes," with six tips, boxed 1940s, Made in USA.

$18-$20

Decorator Set, aluminum with four tips, on blister card, 1960s, Chiltonware, Aluminum Specialty Co., Manitowoc, WI.

$8-$10

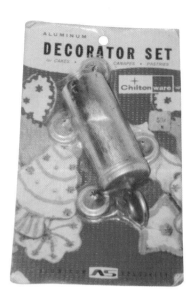

Ateco Decorating Set, six tips with bag, "For cakes, pastries, cookies, etc.," boxed, 1950s, August Thomson Co., New York, NY.

$12-$15

Cake Decorator Bags, Plastic Tips, and Cake and Food Decorating Booklet, boxed, 1950s, Wilton Enterprises, Chicago, IL.

$15-$18

Cooky and Pastry Set, four tips with bags, "For fancy food creations," boxed, 1950s, Kitchen Kapers, Chicago, IL.

$12-$15

Decorating Parchment Sheets, 36 sheets to make decorating bags, boxed, 1950s, Chefmaster Products Co., Chicago, IL.

$10-$12

Sheet Music for "If I Knew You were Coming, I'd 've Baked a Cake," published by Robert Music Corp. 1940s.

$5-$7

This once popular novelty song sung by Eileen Barton has now mostly been lost in time. I did find a copy of the 78 rpm record on Ebay, the B-side is "Poco, Loco in the Coco."

Chapter 10

Pie Pans, Rolling Pins, Cookie & Pastry Presses, Accessories

Pie baking has many dedicated enthusiasts who enjoy the preparation as well as the taste of the final product. Mastering the various steps and techniques is an art, always subject to a special process or step an experienced cook might want to add. Over the years, manufacturers have created numerous pans, rolling pins, presses, crimpers, etc., to help improve results and make the process easier and more fun. Collectors search for unusual or decorative examples and find that a few vintage rolling pins or pastry accessories make great additions to any kitchenware collection.

Saturday Evening Post with cover illustration by Stevan Dohanos. A 1950s mutual swap rest break is shown, pie for milk and milk for pie. Seems like an idyllic exchange to me.

$8-$10

Fire King 9" Pie Plate, "Bake serve store and reheat in the same dish," with label, 1950s, Anchor Hocking, Lancaster, OH.

$15-$20

Bake-King 9" Pie Plate, orange pie recipe, with label, 1950s, Chicago Metallic Mfg. Co., Lake Zurich, IL.

$12-$15

Pyrex Flavor Saver Pie Plate, "Keeps the juice and flavor in your pie!," with label, 1950s, Corning Glass Works, Corning, NY.

$15-$20

Bake-a-Pie, Metal Rim Baking Plates, "Perfect for frozen pies," with label, 1950s, Sutherland Paper Co., Kalamazoo, MI.

$10-$12

Bake-King Save All Pie Plate, "Saves the pie juices, Keeps the oven clean," with label, 1950s.

$12-$15

Pyrex 10" Pie Plate, "bake, serve, freeze, all in one dish," with label, 1960s.

$10-$12

Lattice Pie Cutter, styrene plastic, "Ok'd by experts, Used by housewives, The new modern way to make lattice pies," red on large card, 1950s, Kesco Plastics, Chicago, IL.

$15-$18

Lattice Pie Cutter, styrene plastic, clear with paper label.

$10-$12

"Criss Cross" Lattice Pie-Top Cutter, styrene plastic, "makes perfect lattice–top pies!," in package, 1950s, Clough Products, Prairie Village, KS.

$18-$22

Gold Medal Pie Crimper, metal, "Makes pies the easy way," boxed, 1950s.

$18-$22

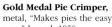

KVP Pie Tape, "Keeps the juice in the pie," boxed, 1950s, Kalamazoo Vegetable Parchment Co., MI.

$10-$12

Ceramic Pie Plates, Apple & Cherry, pie recipes printed under glazing, 1960s.

$12-$15 each

"Bake-an'-Take" Covered Cake Pan, with label, 1950s, Aluminum Specialty Co., Manitowoc, WI.

$15-$18

"Take-a-Long" Covered Pie Pan, with label, 1950s, Aluminum Housewares Corp., St. Louis, MO.

$15-$18

Lokstad Die-cut Rolling Pin, "For cookies, pastries, flatbreads," 1950s, Lokstad Products, Newfolden, MN.

$18-$25

Nayco Ripple Rolling Pin, "For cookies, pies, cakes, and breads," boxed, 1950s.

$25-$30

Munising 17" Rolling Pin, modern design with selected northern hardrock maple, boxed 1940s-1950s.

$22-$25

World's Fair Rolling Pin, "For smooth rolling with a feather touch," with wrapper, 1950s, Forster Mfg. Co., Farmington, ME.

$22-$25

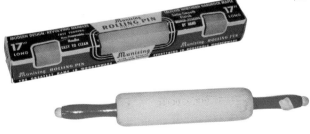

Multiple Roller, "New Type Rolling Pin," styrene plastic, 1950s, Magnus Harmonica Corp., Newark, NJ.

$18-$22

Krispy Krust Rolling Pin, chrome, with catalin plastic handles and ball bearings, 1940s, Buffalo Toy and Tool Works, Buffalo, NY.

$40-$45

Insert Sheet included with "Roll-Rite" Glass Rolling Pin, 1940s.

Glass Rolling Pin, with ribbed handle design, 1930s-1940s.

$20-$25

"Roll-Rite" Glass Rolling Pin, with printed metal end cap, 1940s.

$30-$35

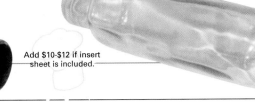

Add $10-$12 if insert sheet is included.

EVERYWOMAN'S

THE WOMAN'S GUIDE TO BETTER LIVING

SEPTEMBER
5¢
1954

HOW TO MAKE YOUR FAVORITE FRUIT PIES

Everywoman's Magazine, September 1954. Covers with only food items, like the favorite fruit pies shown here, were a recurring theme in the 1950s.

$6-$8

Queen Size Rolling Pin,
aluminum with plastic
handles, "Rolls more tender
dough," with label, 1950s-
1960s, Foley Mfg. Co.,
Mnpls, MN.

$22-$25

Ekco Rolling Pin, selected
hardwood, with sleeve,
1950s, Ekco Products Co.,
Chicago, IL.

$15-$20

Ekco Rolling Pin, plastic,
yellow with red and chrome
accents, 1950s.

$30-$35

Ekco Rolling Pin, pink
with green and chrome
accents.

$35-$45

Ekco Rolling Pin,
anodized aluminum, "High
styled for brighter baking,"
boxed, 1950s.

$45-$55

Nevco Rolling Pin,
hardwood with ball
bearings, with label, 1950s,
Nevco Products Inc.,
Yonkers, NY.

$22-$25

Foley Pastry Frame, with
rolling pin cover, wood and
canvas, with label, 1950s,
Foley Mfg. Co., Mnpls, MN.

$22-$25

Ekco Rolling Pin,
hardwood, with label,
1970s.

$12-$15

Happy Home Rolling Pin, hardwood with nylon bearings, with label, 1960s, Woolworth's.

$15-$18

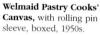

Pastry Cloth and Rolling Pin Cover, "Makes rolling of dough easier and faster than ever before," in package, 1950s, H&P House Furnishing Co., Fairlawn, NJ.

$12-$15

Welmaid Pastry Cooks' Canvas, with rolling pin sleeve, boxed, 1950s.

$10-$12

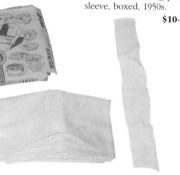

Edith Hansen's Pastry Cloth, with rolling pin coverlet, "A household necessity, Makes baking a pleasure," in package, 1951, The Perflex Co., Shenandoah, IA.

$8-$10

Cookie Sheet Liners, eight liners, "For perfect cookies every time!," in package, 1950s, Superior Insulating Tape Co., St. Louis, MO.

$8-$10

Ateco Magic Cookie Maker, Cake Decorator, "Makes cookies in a jiffy," boxed, 1930s-1940s, August Thomson Co., Brooklyn, NY.

$22-$25

Mirro Cooky & Pastry Press, 15 fancy shapes and wood rack, "Makes 80 cookies in one filling," boxed, 1950s, Mirro Aluminum, Manitowoc, WI.

$22-$25

Ateco Cookie and Noodle Maker, "Stimulate your artistic inclinations,"' boxed, 1950s, August Thomson Co.

$18-$20

COOKIES, CREAM PUFFS, ECLAIRS, LADY FINGERS, MERINGUES

so *Easy* TO MAKE...
AND *Decorate*

"smart cookies. . ."

And smart little sisters, too, to turn out such smart-looking cookies this easy, twist-of-the-wrist way.

The MIRRO Cooky and Pastry Press turns baking touch to magic . . . makes cooky-making a pleasure . . . gives professional results every time.

All sets packaged in colorful display boxes, with dustfree Mylar windows.

MIRRO COOKY-PASTRY PRESS

Just a turn of the handle creates fancy cookies, lady fingers, eclairs, cream puffs or meringue shells

Set contains 12 interchangeable forming plates for making fancy cookies, plus 3 easy-to-use pastry tips. Stain-resisting Alumilite, with lustrous Copper-Tone trim. Comfortable turning grip. Directions and recipes included.

Number	Gauge	Barrel Diam.	Height	Ship. Unit	Weight Ship. Unit
358AM	20	3"	7⅝"	6 only	9 lbs.

Packed in individual 4-color display cartons, then repacked in corrugated shipping carton.

33

Mirro Cooky & Pastry Press as shown in a 1950s catalog.
$18-$20

Simplicity Cooky Press, four designs, "For thick or thin cookies," boxed, 1930s-1940s.

$15-$18

Aluminum Cooky Press, with four forming plates, boxed, 1940s, Made in USA.

$18-$20

Wear-Ever Cookie Press, 12 shapes, "Sensational no-guess measure knob," boxed, 1950s, Aluminum Cooking Utensil Co., New Kensington, PA.

$18-$22

Mirro Cooky Press, "New easy grip, With 12 fancy shapes," boxed, 1940s-1950s, Mirro Aluminum.

$22-$25

Mirro Cooky & Pastry Press, "For cookies, éclairs, cream puffs, etc.," boxed, 1950s, Mirro Aluminum.

$18-$22

Cookie Press and Cake Decorator, "See-It" transparent plastic, boxed, 1950s, Wecolite Co., New York, NY.

$22-$28

Cooky Press, styron plastic, six metal inserts with cake decorator attachments, boxed, 1950s, Popeil Bros., Chicago, IL.

$18-$20

Gadget Master Cookie Press, styrene plastic, "Enjoy making cookies at home," boxed, 1950s, Popeil Bros., Chicago, IL.

$15-$18

Wear-Ever Cookie Gun and Pastry Decorator, with thickness control, boxed, 1960s, Made in Japan for Wear-Ever Aluminum, Chillicothe, OH.

$15-$18

Cookie Chef and Pastry Gun, aluminum and plastic, six design tips, trigger operated, boxed, 1960s, West Bend Aluminum Co., West Bend, WI.

$15-$18

Cookie King, crank-type, cookie press spritz gun, copper-toned aluminum, boxed, 1950s.

$20-$22

Cookie Chef and Pastry Gun, aluminum, "Trig-a-matic," boxed, 1950s, Vital Products Mfg. Co., Cleveland, OH.

$15-$18

Nutbrown Cookie and Biscuit Maker, aluminum, boxed, 1950s, Thos. M. Nutbrown Ltd., Blackpool, England.

$12-$15

Mirro Cookie Kit, "Dial-a-Cookie," pastry press with three rotating disks, makes 12 designs, in package, 1960s, Mirro Aluminum.

$18-$22

Ekco/Mary Ann Cookie and Sandwich Cutter, cuts six different shapes, boxed, 1950s, Ekco Products Co., Chicago, IL.

$12-$15

Wear-Ever "Lazy Suzy" Cookie Cutter Wheel, aluminum with styrene plastic center, "Newest easiest way to make fancy cookies every day," boxed, 1950s, Aluminum Cooking Utensil Co.

$22-$25

Wear-Ever Cookie Gun and Pastry Decorator ad, *McCalls,* November 1957.

$2-$5

Wear-Ever Cookie Gun, "For cookies, biscuits, canapes, with cookie thickness dial, Trigger quick!," boxed, 1950s, Aluminum Cooking Utensil Co.

$18-$22

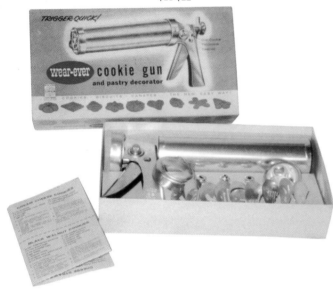

Spry Shortening ad, with 5 on 1 Cookie Cutter Wheel promotion, from *Woman's Day,* November 1953.

$2-$5

Spry Cookie Cutter Wheel Store Placard, 1950s.

$15-$20

Spry Shortening Can, 1950s.

$15-$20

Spry 1950s Cookie Wheel.

$15-$18

Rotating Cookie and Sandwich Cutter, "Cuts five attractive shapes with one easy motion," boxed, 1950s, Overseas Housewares Co., New York, NY.

$15-$18

Mechanical Cookie Cutter, metal, "Cuts dozens of cookies in seconds, No more one at a time!," boxed, 1940s-1950s, Syndicate Sales, Mnpls, MN.

$20-$22

Cookie Cutter Wheel, aluminum with plastic handles, 1950s, Foley Mfg. Co., Mnpls, MN.

$8-$10

Cookie Cutter Wheel, three-shape rotating plastic with wooden handle, 1950s.

$8-$10

The Saturday Evening
POST
February 23, 1957 — 15¢

Victor Borge Tells His Own Story
ROUGHING IT AT MIAMI BEACH
Men Wanted: $25,000 a Year

Saturday Evening Post, September 23, 1957, with cover illustration by Constantin Alajalov. Portly gentleman is shown with heaping plates of food in both hands and no place to sit.

$8-$10

Chapter 11

Cookie Cutters

Collectors find the fun designs and shapes of cookie cutters hard to resist. The earliest cutters were fashioned from small scraps of tin or metal by hand. Manufacturers soon began producing designs to satisfy the needs and wants of users. Through the years, cookie cutters have evolved from all metal forms to stamped aluminum and molded plastic. The variety of shapes available is extensive with sets having illustrative packaging or boxes attracting the most collector interest.

Souvenir Program for the 10th annual Olympia Circus, at the Chicago Stadium, 1942.

$18-$25

The interesting graphics on this program add to its value.

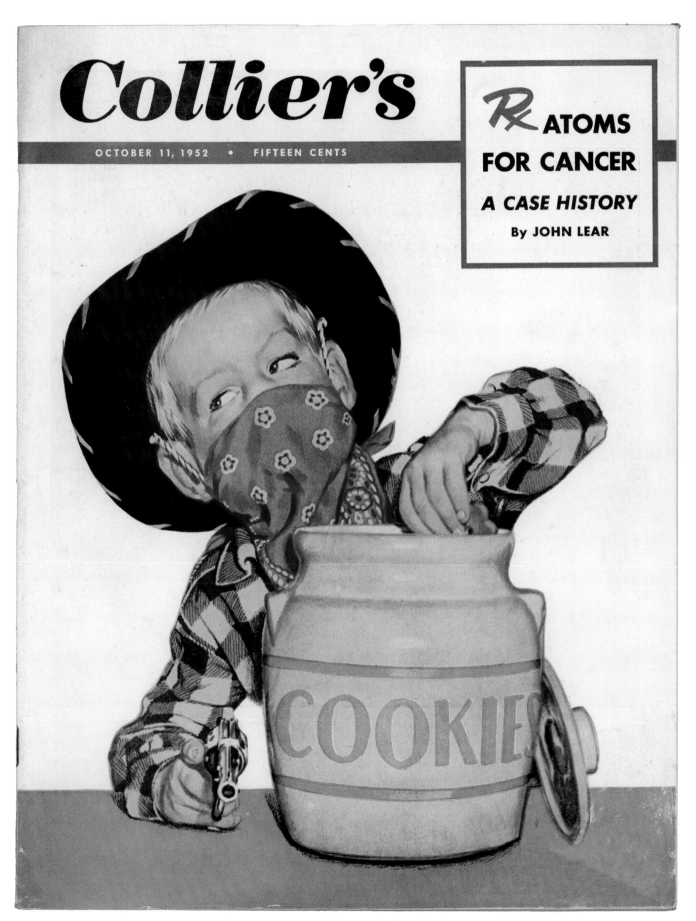

Colliers Magazine, October 11, 1953. This young lad in a cowboy hat makes a humorous image as he tries to hold up a cookie jar. **$8-$10**

Wonder Cutters, 12 assorted metal shapes, "For delightful sandwiches and cookies," boxed, 1930s-1940s, Kreamer Inc., Brooklyn, NY.

$18-$22

Cake and Sandwich Cutters, metal bridge set "for luncheons and card parties," boxed 1930s-1940s.

$15-$20

Cookie Cutters, 12 metal cutters "for all seasons," boxed, 1930s-1940s, GMT Co., New York, NY.

$18-$22

Barnyard Cookie Cutters, 12 metal animal figures, boxed, 1950s.

$18-$22

Old Fashioned Cookie Cutters, 12 metal designs, "For cookies, canapés, etc.," boxed, 1950s.

$18-$22

1950s old-fashioned items were usually designed in the style of the 1890s.

Miniature Cookie Cutters, six metal Christmas designs, boxed, 1950s.

$12-$15

Miniature Cookie Cutters, six metal designs, boxed, 1950s.

$12-$15

Patriotic Cookie Cutters, four metal designs, "For celebrations and parties," boxed, 1950s.

$25-$30

Trick or Treat Cookie Cutters, six metal Halloween designs, boxed, Ateco, August Thomson Co., New York, NY.

$40-$45

Easter Cookie Cutters, six metal designs, "Also for cheese, thin breads, etc.," boxed, 1950s, Ateco, August Thomson Co., New York, NY.

$18-$22

"Tala" Cookie Cutters, 12 metal shapes, boxed, 1950s, Taylor Law & Co. Ltd., Stourbridge, England.

$18-$20

Cookie Cutter, 2 in 1, Snow Man or Gingerbread Boy, metal 8 in. high, "For all party occasions," boxed, 1950s.

$18-$20

Cookie Cutter, Santa Claus, metal 8 in. high, "For all Christmas occasions," boxed, 1950s.

$18-$22

Baking Sheet with Holiday Cookies Label, 1950s, Bake King, Chicago Metallic Mfg. Co., Chicago.

$18-$22

Mirro Cookie Cutters, "In popular designs," in package, 1950s-1960s, Mirro Aluminum, Manitowoc, WI.

$12-$15

Mirro Gingerbread Man, color-tone aluminum, on card, 1950s, Mirro Aluminum.

$18-$22

Mirro Fairy Tale Cookie Cutter Set, five pieces, color-tone aluminum, on blister card, 1950s, Mirro Aluminum.

$18-$20

Holiday Cookie Cutters, five aluminum shapes, on card, 1950s, Color Craft, Indianapolis, IN.

$18-$22

Mirro Cookie Cutters, six aluminum shapes, "In popular designs," in package, 1950s, Mirro Aluminum.

$18-$20

Character cookie cutter sets with colorful graphics appeal to collectors.

Hansel and Gretel Cookie Cutter Set, five pieces, styrene plastic, boxed, 1947, Educational Products Co., New York, NY.

$35-$45

Christmas Cookie Cutter Set, nine pieces, plastic in holiday shapes, boxed, 1950s, Educational Products Co.

$22-$25

This six-sided box made a handy storage container, so many were saved.

Plastic Cookie Cutters, eight-piece set with figural animal shapes, boxed, 1940s, Hutzler Mfg. Co., Long Island City, NY.

$35-$40

"Big Four" Cookie Cutters or "Big 6" Cookie Cutters, in package, Hutzler Mfg. Co.

1950s (first two from left)

$15-$18

1960s (at right)

$12-$15

3-D Cookie Cutter Set, eight plastic cutters make four animal-shaped cookies, 'That really stand up," boxed, 1950s, Wecolite Co., New York, NY.

$18-$22

Circus Cookie Cutter Set, nine pieces, plastic, boxed, 1950s, Educational Products Co.

$35-$40

A single cutter was also available.

Multi-Matic Cookie Cutter and Ice Cube Maker, "Cuts clever cookies instantly," deluxe set with two cutters, boxed, 1950s.

$25-$28

"Frigee-Maid" Ice Box Cookie Molds, "easy to store, slice, and bake," boxed, 1950s, Flambeau Plastics Corp., Baraboo, WI.

$22-$25

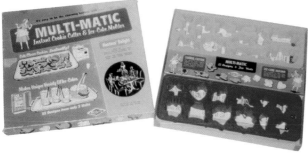

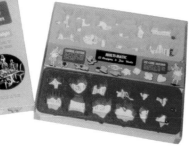

Refriger-Mold, Ice Box Cookie Maker, two pieces, styrene plastic, "anyone can make refrigerator or rolled cookies," boxed, 1950s, The Gladd Co., Mnpls, MN.

$12-$15

Chapter 12

Measuring Spoons and Cups, Timers, Scales, and Adders

Measurement aids are a practical kitchen accessory. Cooks need to know how much of an ingredient to use, or have a way to time a cooking process. Many varieties of measuring cups, spoons, timers, and scales have been produced over the years, and manufacturers were quick to adapt features that set their products apart. Measuring sets were bound together or a wall rack was provided to make them handier to use; special designs, such as adjustable models or double-sided wet and dry measures, were created.

Many companies added color or novel design shapes to increase interest. Collectors today will find a range of vintage measures, timers, and scales of interest, and can concentrate on examples that match their other kitchen collectibles.

Saturday Evening Post, February 19, 1955. This cover, by Amos Sewell, shows an eager group of kids making a raid on a well-stocked refrigerator.
$8-$10

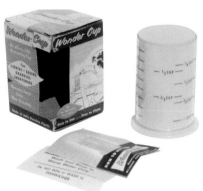

Wonder Cup, plastic measuring device, "For the particular housewife, takes the guesswork and messwork out of cooking," boxed, 1950s, Milmour Products, Chicago, IL.

$12-$15

Measurettes, four "spun ray" aluminum measuring cups, boxed, 1950s.

$15-$18

Kitchen Gift Set, deluxe set with measuring spoons and cups, S&P shakers, and mixer, boxed, 1950s, Color Craft, Indianapolis, IN.

$85-$95

Tallscoops Measuring Spoons, four colored aluminum spoons with rack, "a bright addition to any kitchen," boxed, 1954, Ray Walther Co., Des Moines, IA.

$35-$45

These spoons also appeal to collectors of colored aluminum items.

"Long 'n' Lovely" Measure Set, aluminum with plastic-coated handles, "they're simply beautiful and so handy," on card, 1950s, Magic Hostess Corp., Kansas City, MO.

$25-$30

Tala Cooks Measure Funnel, aluminum with printed design, 1950s, Taylor Law & Co. Ltd., Stourbridge, England.

$18-$20

Miniature graduated revere pan could be used as a measuring cup or a child's toy, the one shown was a bank promotion piece.

Revere Ware Measuring Cup, boxed, 1950s, Revere Copper and Brass Inc., Rome Mfg. Div., Rome, NY.

$18-$22

Mirro Measuring Spoon Set, color-tone aluminum, on blister card, 1950s-1960s, Mirro Aluminum, Manitowoc, WI.

$15-$18

in this July *issue...*

**new
summer cookbook**
188 recipes—62 menus

woman's day
THE A & P MAGAZINE **7** *cents*

PLUS
"1 day's cooking:
3 days' eating"

Woman's Day, July 1955. This laughing young lady has taken the
idea of juggling kitchen activities to new heights.

$6-$8

Ekco/Mary Ann Cooking and Measuring Set, four pieces, aluminum, boxed, 1940s-1950s, Ekco Products Co., Chicago, IL.

$18-$22

Scoop Set, four pieces, mirror-finish aluminum, boxed, 1950s, Made in W. Germany by Westmark. Overseas Housewares Co., New York, NY.

$18-$20

Measuring Cups, aluminum with plastic handles, 1960s.

$12-$15

Teapot Hot Pad Holder, styrene plastic, 1950s.

$15-$18

Rooster Measuring Spoon and Hot Pad Holder, styrene plastic, with spoons, 1950s.

$22-$25

Measuring Spoons, four pieces, multicolor plastic, 1950s.

$8-$12 each

A manufacturer's mark will add to its value.

Geese Measuring Cups, four-piece set, plastic with colored beaks and eyes, 1950s-1960s.

$18-$22

Measuring Cups, four pieces, multicolor polyethylene plastic, 1950s-1960s, Hutzler Mfg. Co., Long Island City, NY.

$12-$15

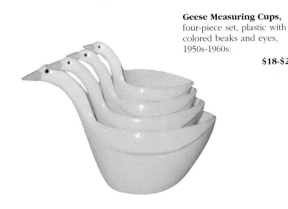
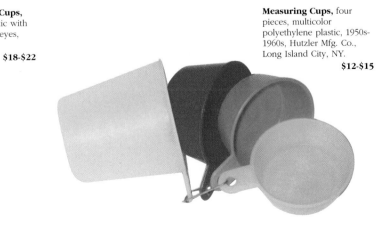

Lustro-Ware Measuring Spoons, styrene plastic, 1950s.

$15-$18

Measuring Cup Set, four pieces, styrene plastic, "An indispensable utensil for canning," 1950s, Shel-Glo, Kilgore Mfg. Co.

$12-$15

Lux Minute Minder, boxed, 1950s, Robert Shaw Controls Co., Waterbury, CT.

$18-$20

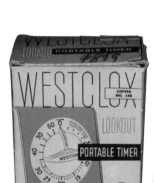

Mirro Matic Kitchen Timer, "counts the minutes when minutes count," boxed, 1950s, Mirro Aluminum.

$22-$25

Maid of Honor Household Timer, no winding necessary, boxed, 1950s, sold only by Sears Roebuck & Co.

$20-$22

Mirro Matic Timer, gold-toned aluminum, 1950s, Mirro Aluminum.

$15-$18

Westclox Portable Timer, copper and plastic. boxed, 1950s, Westclox, General Time Corp., LaSalle, IL.

$18-$22

American Family Scale, with food graphics and plastic weigh platform, 1960s-1970s.

$18-$20

SMALL HOME

BUILDERS *Year Book*

3rd Annual Edition
of 1,000,000 copies

WORLD'S FAIR EDITION
TWENTY-FIVE CENTS

Featuring—
N. Y. WORLD'S FAIR
#1 DEMONSTRATION HOME
AND 30 OTHER SMALL
HOMES OF TOMORROW

WILBUR LUMBER CO.
"WHERE YOUR HOME BEGINS"
PHONE: GReenfield 1210   WEST ALLIS, WIS.   7919 W. NATIONAL AVE.

THIS EDITION 1,000,000 COPIES

Small Home Builders Year Book, 1939. Cover illustration shows couple gazing into a crystal ball to view their home of the future. Magazine features a demonstration home from the 1939 New York's World's Fair.

$8-$10

American Family Scale, metal with gray and white dial, 1950s, American Family Scale Co., Chicago.

$15-$18

Kitchen Scale, aluminum top bowl with plastic bottom, marked "House Proud," registered design, 1950s.

$22-$28

Kitchen Scale, plastic with metal top and front, 1948, Hanson Scale Co., Northbrook, IL.

$15-$18

"Add-It" Adding Machine, "Dial-A-Matic adds and subtracts, Quick, easy, accurate," boxed, 1950s, Sterling Plastics Co., Union, NJ.

$15-$18

Super Add-A-Matic Supermarket Adder, 1950s.

$10-$12

"Dan-Dee" Add-kwik Supermarket Adder, in package, 1950s.

$15-$18

Chapter 13

Strainers, Presses, Etc.

S trainers are a kitchen aid to process or liquefy solid foods. They are also used to make applesauce, purees, etc. They vary in complexity from simple handheld wire mesh units, to versions with a separate mashing element or mechanical plunger action. Presses for hamburgers aided in forming convenient, uniform patties that could be frozen for later use. Strainers and presses vary from early primitive models to those of more recent manufacture. Unusual examples, and those having colorful original packaging, are of most interest to collectors.

Aldon Products ad from *House Furnishing Review*, July 10, 1948.

"Nox-Lab," adjustable strainer, stainless steel, boxed, 1930s, Knox Laboratories, Knox, IN.

$18-$20

Salad & Fruit Washer, collapsible, with label, 1960s, Made in Japan.

$15-$18

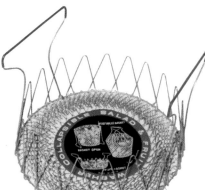

"In-Genia" Vegetable Steam Basket, "Makes any pot a double boiler," boxed, 1950s, Overseas Housewares Co., New York, NY.

$12-$15

SteaMarvel Steamer, metal, "Safe and sanitary, saves vitamins," boxed, 1960s-1970s, Aero Industrial Co., Burbank, CA.

$10-$12

Metal Ricer and Press, with stand and wood wedging element, 1930s-1940s.

$15-$18

Ricer or Juicer, cast metal, 1930s.
large $18-$22
small $12-$15

Jel-Aid, "The answer to the jelly straining problem," boxed, 1940s-1950s, Huot Mfg. Co., St Paul, MN.

$18-$22

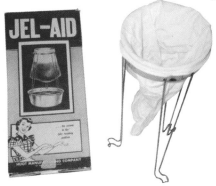

Handy Fruit Press & Potato Ricer, with sleeve, 1950s, Handy Things Mfg. Co., Ludington, MI.

$22-$25

"Slice-a-Slice" Bread Slicer, metal apparatus holds a bread slice in place, so it can be sliced again for thin party sandwiches, canapés, etc. Boxed, 1940s-1950s deluxe set with knife, Aldon Products Co., Duncannon, PA.

$20-$22

"Slice-a-Slice" Bread Slicer, boxed unit alone.

$15-$18

"Chef" Hamburger Patty Press, aluminum, "Quick, easy, sanitary," boxed, 1950s, Chef Products Co., Elkhart, IN.

$20-$25

Deluxe Hamburger Press, chrome plated, "For kitchen, patio, and barbecue use," boxed, 1950s, Kitchen Quip Inc., Waterloo, IN.

$12-$15

Jumbo Hamburger Press, wood with painted rooster design, boxed, 1950s, Western Woods Inc., Portland, OR.

$22-$25

"Form 'N Fry" Hamburger Press, aluminum plunger action, "Easy to use, Saves time too," boxed, 1950s, David Douglas & Co. Inc., Manitowoc, WI.

$12-$15

Villaware Juicer/Strainer Set, polypropylene, two-piece juicer with bowl, in package, 1960s-1970s.

$8-$10

This juicer is usually missing its bowl.

Strainer, styrene plastic with integral metal mesh, 1950s, Plasmetl, Chicago, IL.

$12-$15

Chapter 14

Graters, Shredders, Slicers

Graters and shredders perform similar functions. Graters are better suited for cheese, chocolates, and harder foods, while shredders are usually reserved for lettuce or cabbage. Slicers are often used for tomatoes, potatoes, cheese, and similar foods. Most graters and shredders have a pattern of sharp-edged holes for producing fine, medium, or coarse food depending on the size of the hole. Slicers usually have a thin, sharp metal slot or wire to perform the cutting action. Devices range in complexity from simple handheld units to rotating tabletop models with interchangeable blade elements. A wide variety of graters, shredders, and slicers were produced over the years, with many companies offering special features or designs to have a competitive edge. Original boxes usually provided helpful instructions and recipes, and many were saved through the years. They typically feature interesting graphics and are sought after by collectors.

Saturday Evening Post, November 10, 1956, with cover illustration by Constantin Alajalov. A seat of gabbing girlfriends is shown eating to their hearts content, while the matronly lady walking by doesn't seem to be very interested in the dietary fare on her own tray.
$8-$10

The Saturday Evening **POST** November 10, 1956 — 15¢

My Life in the White House Doghouse
By DREW PEARSON

"In-Genia" Folding Grater,
with attached tray, "the
greatest little grater you
ever used," boxed, 1950s,
Made in Italy, Overseas
Housewares Co., New York,
NY.

$15-$18

**Standfast Grating and
Shredding Utensil,** plastic
with metal grating inserts,
"the only shredder that
doesn't fight back," boxed,
1950s,Standfast Products
Co., Cleveland, OH.

$22-$28

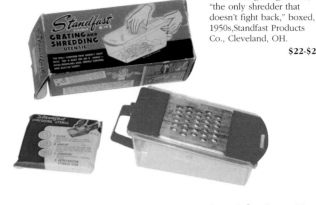

Grater and Pan Set, "Grate
right into the pan," boxed,
1950s, Elpo Industries Inc.,
New York, NY.

$15-$18

Acme Safety Grater, "For
easy dicing, grating,
straining," with insert sheet,
1950s, Acme Metal Goods
Co., Newark, NJ.

$12-$15

Vitex Safety Grater,
styrene plastic, "grate with
safety," boxed 1940s-1950s,
a Renwal Product.

$15-$18

Plasti-Grate, safe, sanitary,
stainless, with attached
card, 1950s, Nu-dell Mfg.
Co., Chicago, IL.

$12-$15

Streamline Utility Cutter,
metal, "saves time, saves
energy,'" boxed, 1930s-
1940s, Modern Home
Utilities, Chicago, IL.

$22-$28

**Nu-Age Shredder
Slicer,** Grater, stainless
steel, "Fully adjustable,"
boxed, 1950s, New-Age
Products Co., Brooklyn, MI.

$18-$22

Rapid Salad Set, three pieces, metal, "Shreds, slices, grates," boxed, 1930s, Bluffton Slaw Cutter Co., Bluffton, OH.

$18-$22

Bromwell's Greater Grater, "Easy to use, For all grating purposes." with paper label, 1930s, Bromwell Wire Goods Mfg. Co., Cincinnati, OH.

$12-$15

Rotary Food Grater, metal with wood handle, "It grates so many things in a jiffy" boxed, 1950s, Lorraine Novelty Mfg. Co., New York, NY.

$15-$18

Safety Grate 'n Shred, styrene plastic, "Safe, compact, easy to clean," boxed, 1950s, Popeil Bros, Chicago, IL.

$18-$22

Knapp's Safety Veg-e-grater, metal, boxed, 1930s, Knapp Monarch Co., Belleville, IL.

$18-$22

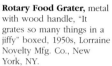

Sliding rack separates user's hand from cutting element.

Rapid Salad Set, metal, "Shreds, slices, grates, no slip, slide, or muss," boxed, 1950s, Bluffton Slaw Cutter Co., Bluffton, OH.

$18-$20

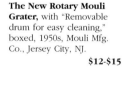

Artbeck Dial-a-matic Shredder, "Easy, safe, at the turn of a dial," boxed, 1950s, Arthur Beck Co., Chicago, IL.

$18-$22

The New Rotary Mouli Grater, with "Removable drum for easy cleaning," boxed, 1950s, Mouli Mfg. Co., Jersey City, NJ.

$12-$15

Slice-a-Way Shredder & Slicer, plastic unit with, "3-way adjustable metal blade," boxed, 1950s, Popeil Bros, Chicago, IL.

$12-$15

Feemster's Famous Vegetable Slicer, metal with adjustable platform, boxed 1940s-1950s, W.R. Feemster Co., Brooklyn, MI.

$15-$18

Speedy All Purpose Slicer, "Faster, easier, amazing new kitchen aid," boxed, 1950s, Tower Hall, Chicago, IL.

$12-$15

Deluxe Dial-O-Matic Food Cutter, plastic with metal blade, "Slices, shreds, waffles, performs miracles with food," boxed, 1958, Popeil Bros, Chicago, IL.

$18-$22

Mouli Salad Maker, metal with rotating grater elements, "Slices, chops, shreds," boxed, 1950s, Mouli Mfg. Co., Jersey City, NJ.

$18-$20

Tupperware Grater and Bowl, 1970s.

$10-$12.

Grater attachment could be replaced with a lid for storage. This is a common Tupperware kitchen accessory.

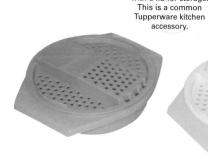

Slicer and Grater, plastic, 1950s-1960s, Linda Foursome, made in USA.

$6-$8

Chapter 15

Potato Cutters, Choppers, Corers, Etc.

S pecialty cutters, choppers, and corers provide useful kitchen functions, including making french-fries, dicing onions and vegetables, coring apples and fruits, etc. Numerous examples were produced by manufacturers and innovative marketers through the years, and many of these same products continue to be made in modern versions today. Examples include rotating food choppers from the 1950s, and one-piece apple corers that could core and section an apple in one motion. Choppers and cutters appeal to kitchenware collectors who want a variety of objects having a specialized purpose.

Collier's Magazine, November 2, 1946, with cover illustration by Jon Whitcomb. The young folks on the cover will probably have a hard time with this apple. They should try one of the apple gadgets shown in this section. **$8-$10**

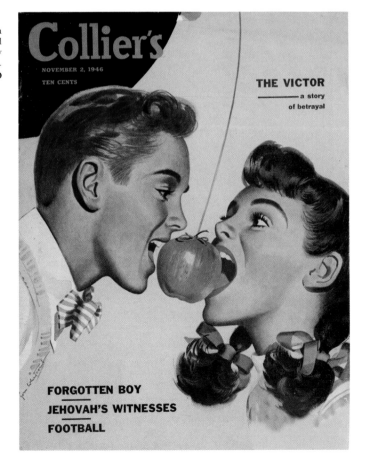

The New Villa French Fry Potato Cutter, metal with wood handle, "Strongest and safest," boxed, 1940s, Made in England.

$22-$25

Blitzhacker Lightning Food Chopper, plastic with metal cutting blade, "Does the job just by tapping, Original Swiss design," boxed, 1950s, New-Nel Kitchen Products, Chicago, IL.

$18-$22

Maid of Honor French Fry Potato Cutter, metal with wood handle, "Fast, convenient," boxed, 1950s, Sold only by Sears Roebuck & Co.

$18-$20

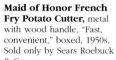

Mrs. Damar's Potato Cutter, metal with natural wood handle, "Cuts 25 french fries in one stroke," boxed, 1950s, Damar Products Co., Newark, NJ.

$20-$22

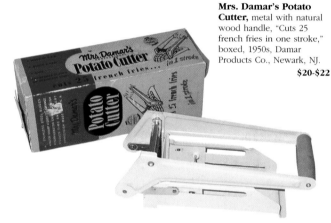

Ekco French Fry Potato Cutter, metal with plastic handle, 1960s
Ekco Products Co., Chicago, IL.

$8-$12

Presto French Fry Cutter, metal, "Cuts a whole potato at one time, safe as a simple toy," with attached card, 1950s, M.E. Houck, Cincinnati, OH.

$10-$12

Nutbrown Chipper and French Fry Cutter, metal with wooden handles, simple to operate, "The finest of all chippers!," boxed, 1940s, Thos. M. Nutbrown Ltd., Blackpool, England.

$25-$28

Huot Serrater and Meat Tenderizer, stainless steel with plastic handle, "Give your salads a new zip," with sleeve 1950s, Huot Mfg. Co., St Paul, MN.

$15-$18

"Chop-o-matic" Food Chopper, plastic with automatic rotating stainless steel blades, "Just tap it," boxed, 1956, Popeil Bros, Chicago, IL.

$18-$22

Ron Popeil demonstrated this chopper on TV in the 1950s, and revolutionized the selling of kitchen gadgets.

The Avon Giant Size Rotomatic Food Chopper, plastic with stainless steel blades, boxed, 1950s, Avon Products Co.

$20-$22

Sky-line Miracle Chopper, automatically rotating stainless steel blades, boxed, 1950s.

$20-$22

A product of the Prestige Group, made in England.

Roto Chop, giant automatic food chopper, "Steel blades rotate as they chop," boxed, 1958, Popeil Bros, Chicago, IL.

$18-$20

Tearless Onion, Vegetable, and Nut Chopper, metal and wood top with glass cup, with label 1940s-1950s, Acme Metal Goods Mfg. Co.

$18-$20

Chopper, Vegetable and Nut Meats, decorated metal and wood top with graduated glass container, 1950s.

$12-$15

Automatic Food Chopper, metal and plastic top with graduated glass container, 1950s.

$12-$15

Food Chopper, plastic with steel blades, 1950s.

$12-$15

Tearless Onion and Vegetable Chopper, stainless steel blades, metal and wood knob with glass container, with label, 1940s-1950s, Acme Metal Goods Mfg. Co., Newark, NJ.

$15-$18

Merry Go Round Food Chopper, plastic with wood top knob, 1950s.

$12-$15

Federal Onion Choppers, regular, painted metal with wooden knob, graduated, with label, 1940s
$25-$28

Deluxe, perforated aluminum top with wooden knob, graduated, with label, 1940s
$28-$35

"Chop' n Slice," **Chopper,** stainless steel, "Slices, dices, chops," on blister card, 1964, Made in Japan for Nevco, Yonkers, NY.
$8-$10

Kitchen Chopper, stainless steel, "Comfortable, natural grip," with insert card, 1950s.
$10-$12

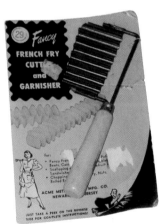

Food Chopper, stainless steel blades with wooden handle, 1940s.
$12-$15

Fancy French Fry Cutter and Garnisher, metal with wooden handle, on card, 1950s, Acme Metal Goods Mfg. Co., Newark, NJ.
$12-$15

This was my first collectible gadget.

Chopper, Stainless Steel with Plastic Handle, "Meat tenderizer, chopper, dicer," with sleeve, 1950s, The Turner and Seymour Mfg. Co., Torrington, CT.
$18-$22

Kwik-Kut "The ideal food chopper," stainless steel with tooth edge, boxed, 1950s, Kwik-Kut Mfg. Co., Mohawk, NY
$10-$12

Apple Slicer-Corer, "an apple a day keeps the doctor away," on card, 1960, by Ludwig Mfg. Co., Racine, WI.

$12-$15

Apple and Pear Corer, Slicer, metal, "Makes fruit serving a pleasure," on card, 1950s, Turner and Seymour Mfg. Co.

$12-$15

Apple Slicer and Corer, metal, "Eight slices in one stroke," on card, 1976, Kitchen King, Central Islip, NY.

$6-$8

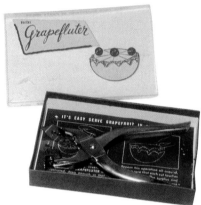

The Grapefluter, metal, "It's easy to serve grapefruit in party dress," boxed, 1950s, G.M.Thurnauer, New York, NY.

$18-$20

This company was a pioneer in the kitchen gadget field.

Hostess Wire Slicer, metal slices thick or thin, the, "All purpose slicer for cheese, butter, eggs, etc.," on card, 1960, A Kenberry Product, John Clark Brown Inc., Belleville, NJ.

$12-$15

Cheese Slicer, rust proof metal and plastic, "For butter, eggs, and many others," on card, 1950s, Vaughan Mfg. Co., Chicago, IL.

$12-$15

Cheese Slicer, stainless steel with easy grip wooden handle, "Ideal for ice cream, butter, bananas, eggs, etc.," on card, 1950s, The Turner and Seymour Mfg. Co., Torrington, CT.

$15-$18

The Kwik Kut Cheese Slicer, metal and wood, "Slices butter, ice cream, eggs, etc.," on card, 1950s, Uebel Mfg. Co., Bellevue, KY.

$12-$15

Citra Grapefruit Corer, serrated stainless steel with wooden handle, on card, 1950s, Citra Products, Winter Haven, FL.

$15-$18

Real-a-Peel Parer and Corer, metal, "The household knife of many uses," on card, 1940s-1950s Tarrson Co., Chicago, IL.

$15-$18

Bean-X, "Stems, strings, slices, beans stay greener, taste better," boxed, 1950s, G.N. Coughlan Mfg. Co., West Orange, NJ.

$10-$15

Vitex Corer, for fruits and vegetables, plastic with wooden handle, "Makes the fruit appear delightfully attractive & appetizing," boxed, 1950s. A Renwal Product, made in USA.

$10-$12

Rosebud Radish Cutter, styrene plastic, "Makes radish roses simply and easily—no skill needed," on card, 1950s, Nudell Plastics.

$12-$15

Saw Knife, miracle stainless steel serrated edge, "For frozen food, poultry, etc.," boxed, 1950s, Saw Knife Co., Chicago, IL.

$8-$10

Kitchen Tested Wonder Knife, "Never needs sharpening," on card, 1950s, Another Lifetime Cutlery Product.

$12-$15

Home Smorgasbord Knife, "Beautiful design with Swedish steel blade," boxed, 1950s, Simmons Slicing Knife Co., Chicago, IL.

$12-$15

Amazing Peel King, electric peeler with stainless steel blades, pares, peels, slices, etc., "Wife saver, does the work for you!," boxed, 1950s-1960s, S&H Mfg. Co., Cleveland, OH.

$25-$35

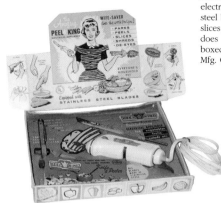

Another amazing thing about this peeler is that a separate massager attachment was available.

Gadget Master Grapefruit Knife, stainless steel with plastic handle, "For preparing grapefruit and orange segments," on card, 1950s, Popeil Bros, Chicago, IL.

$18-$20

Vitex Grapefruit Preparer, plastic, "Ideal for sectioning," boxed, 1950s, A Renwal Product.

$8-$10

Duol Frozen Food Knife, stainless steel, "The perfect kitchen robot, does everything, cuts, saws, slices, serves!," boxed, 1950s.

$12-$15

Blue Ribbon Carving Set, stainless steel with stag-pattern handle, boxed, 1950s.

$18-$22

Famous Coronet Carving Set, stainless steel with plastic handles. boxed, 1950s, E.C.L., New York, NY.

$18-$20

4-Waynife, stainless steel with plastic handle, "World's most versatile kitchen knife," on card 1950s.

$12-$15

Veri-Sharp, stainless kitchen cutlery, with a Wondawood handle, on card, 1960 Imperial Knife Co., Providence, RI.

$8-$10

Households Serrated Paring Knife, stainless steel with hardwood handle, on card, 1950s.

$8-$10

Lightning Action Ice-Cream Scoop, stainless with plastic handle, 'A necessity for the smart housewife.' boxed, 1950s, Kam kap Inc., New York, NY.

$35-$45

Bi-Cor Ice-Cream Scoop, stainless with plastic handle, "For ice cream, potatoes, sandwiches," boxed, 1950s, Bloomfield Industries, Chicago, IL.

$20-$25

Scoop Master Ice-Cream Scoop, "For modern serving, for every kitchen," boxed, 1950s, Bonny Products Co., New York, NY.

$35-$45

Ice-cream scoops with their original box are a collector favorite.

Ice-Cream Scoop, plastic with push button ejector, 1950s, Lloyd Disher Co., Decatur, IL.

$12-$15

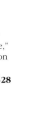

Quick Mayonnaise Maker, steel with glass housing, "Made expressly for the Wesson Oil people," boxed 1940s-1950s, Wesson Oil, New Orleans, LA.

$25-$28

Automatic Butter Curler, two-piece metal unit, boxed, 1960s, Made in Japan for Chadwick Miller.

$10-$12

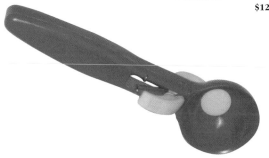

Saucy Melter, melts butter, cheese, sauces, "No scorching, No burning, No watching," boxed, 1950s-1960s, Aluminum Housewares Corp., St Louis, MO.

$12-$15

Shrimpmaster, plastic and metal, "No drudgery, no tired fingers, no ruined shrimp," boxed, 1950s.

$12-$15

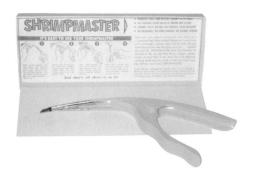

Chapter 16

Barbecue Tools, Aprons, Accessories & Miscellaneous

Barbecue items helped promote the all American activity of the backyard cookout. These products produced in the 1950s for a growing suburban marketplace usually have a whimsical or humorous viewpoint. At most cookouts, the chef played a center-stage role. It was only natural that he or she should wear an entertaining or humorous smock to help enliven the activities. Other products such as tool sets, and barbecue accessories had a similar impact, adding to their appeal. Collectors today look for unusual or interesting items with fanciful designs that help recall the 1950s era.

Page from the *Kipp Brothers catalog* depicting several barbeque sets.

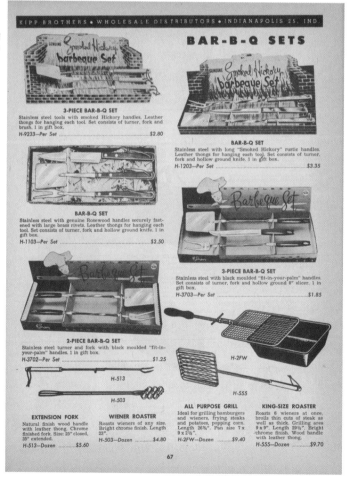

Everywoman's Magazine, July 1955. Here's a great scene of pre-cookout preparation 1950s style. The admiring looks could be due to the chef's first prize ribbon, although not for this meal, it hasn't been cooked yet!   **$6-$8**

Wienie Wheel, aluminum rotating grill attachment, "A California product for zestful living," boxed, 1950s, Wil-Nor Products, Tarzana, CA.

$15-$18

Shish Kabab, aluminum rotating grill attachment, boxed, 1950s, Wil-Nor Products, Tarzana, CA.

$15-$18

Bar-B-Q Tumble Basket, "For the best in greaseless outdoor charcoal cooking," with insert card 1950s.

$18-$22

Bar-B-Skews and Twin Bar-B-Skews, "For outdoor and indoor cooking," on card, M.E. Houck, 'The House of Kitchen Gadgets', Cincinnati, OH.

large **$12-$15**

small **$6-$8**

Picnic or Barbecue as shown in a 1950s *Top Value Stamps Catalog.*

$12-$15

Longhorn Meat Markers, 12 metal cooking level markers, boxed, 1950s, Bar & Barbecue Products, Los Angeles, CA.

$15-$18

Skotch O' matic Hot or Cold Jug, metal and plastic, 1/2 gal, "Press the bulb, it serves a drink, a delight to use!," boxed, 1950s, Hamilton- Skotch Corp., Hamilton, OH.

$30-$35

Spiffy Jug, insulated metal with plastic lid, was also made in green & blue, 1950s, Hamilton-Skotch Corp.

$22-$25

This jug helped inspire me when I was trying to name this book.

Skotch Picnic Kooler, Insulated metal with lid and plastic tray for dry foods, 1950s, Hamilton-Skotch Corp.

$22-$25

Condition is important on this frequently seen cooler.

Skotch Ice, cans of freezable liquid were reusable ice cubes, "Keeps food and drink cold, the dry way—no messy melting," in package, 1950s, Hamilton-Skotch Corp.

$18-$22

Barbecue Set, five pieces, chrome plated with wooden handles, boxed, 1950s.

$25-$35

Instant Charcoal Grill, "No lighter fluid needed, take anywhere," 1950s-1960s, E-Z-Por Corp., "Products for better living," Chicago, IL.

$15-$18

Barbecue Tool Set, stainless steel with "No-slip safety handles, For the outdoor chef," boxed, 1950s, Washington Forge.

$25-$35

Arthur Godfrey Barbecue, with charcoal inside, "The charcoal pit for broiling your food," with cardboard insert, 1950s, Marc Mfg. Co., Chicago, IL.

$28-$35

Arthur Godfrey endorsed a number of products in the 1950s, this disposable barbecue is seldom seen today.

Clyde Bar-B-Q Set, deluxe three-piece stainless steel set with wooden handles, boxed, 1950s, Clyde Cutlery Co., Clyde, OH.

$20-$22

Androck Barbecue Salt & Pepper Shakers, stainless steel and wood with leather hangers, 1950s, The Washburn Co., Worcester MA and Rockford, IL.

$15-$18

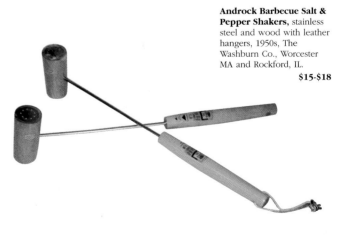

Household's Barbecue Set, deluxe, three pieces, boxed Household Mfg. Co., Hawthorne, CA.

$20-$22

Gril-Lite Charcoal Lighter, "For quick starting of charcoal and wood fires," 1950s.

$10-$12

Sweet Apple-Wood Smoke Flakes, 1950s, Patrick Cudahy Inc., Cudahy, WI.

$12-$15

Barbecue Apron Set, "I'm an old chow hand!,". 4 piece, mitts, apron, and hat, 1950s, Parvin Mfg. Co., Los Angeles, CA.

$22-$25

Aprons with a comical design were a fun 1950s barbecue accessory, probably arising from the fact that men rarely prepared food at other times.

Nuttin To It!, "hand printed for bar and barbecue, styled in California,". in package, 1950s.

$18-$22

Barbecue Aprons, "Dig This Crazy Apron," heavy duty, hand painted, in package, 1950s, Parvin Mfg. Co.

$18-$22

Chromalox Electric Barbecue Lighter, "Fast, safe, odorless," boxed, 1950s, Chromalox, Murfreesboro, TN.

$15-$18

Keeping these mitts in the package protects you from exposure to asbestos.

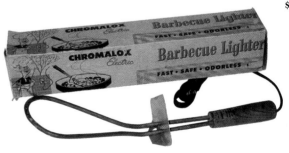

Broil-A-Foil, disposable aluminum broiler pans, "Gets rid of the messiest job in the kitchen," boxed, 1950s-1960s, Metal Foil Products Mfg. Co., Linden, NJ.

$8-$10

Tuck, "Durable heavy plastic tablecloth, for parties and picnics," boxed, 1950s, Technical Tape Corp., New Rochelle, NY.

$8-$10

Androck Steak Broiler, metal, "For outdoor appetites," with insert card, 1950s, The Washburn Co.

$12-$15

Kloth Klips, set of four metal tablecloth clips, "For gracious outdoor living," Acme Metal Goods Mfg. Co., Newark, NJ. This example was found in an antiques store in Peru, IN.

$12-$15

Shish-ka-bab-eez, metal set of two, "For a real sensational cooking experience," boxed, 1950s, Beacon Metal Products, Chicago, IL.

$15-$18

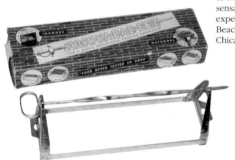

Better Homes and Gardens Barbecue Book, hard cover, 1956, Meredith Publishing Co., Des Moines, Iowa.

$8-$10

Great cover graphics, such as these, add to collector interest.

Big Boy Barbecue Book, "Shows how easy it is to cook on spit or grill," soft cover, 1956, Kitchen Recipe Institute, New York, NY.

$8-$10

Snack Toaster, metal with wood handles, "Toasted sealed sandwiches, America's new taste delight," boxed, 1950s, Federal Mfg. & Engr. Corp., Brooklyn, NY.

$18-$22

Popeil's Toastette, metal with wooden handles, "Tasty sandwich pies for all occasions," boxed, 1950s, Popeil Bros, Chicago, IL.
$18-$22

Toas-Tite, metal with wood handles, "Makes a delicious sealed in drip proof hot toasted sandwich," boxed, 1950s, Bar-B-Buns, Inc., Cincinnati, OH.
$18-$22

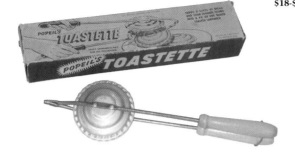

Sandwich Toaster, metal with wooden handles, 1950s, Thos. M. Nutbrown Ltd., Blackpool, England.
$12-$15

Wolff Visible Toaster, metal, "Makes toast as you like it," boxed, 1940s-1950s either version.
$12-$15

Wolff Visible Toaster, metal, "Makes toast as you like it," boxed, 1940s-1950s either version
$12-$15

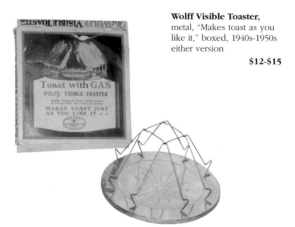

Swift's Premium ad with Sandwich Toaster offer, from *Family Circle,* June 1950.
$2-$5

Sandwich Toasters were a 1950s gadget that allowed you to put bread, meat, cheese, etc. into a hinged metal cooking unit and toast the contents over a stove or campfire.

Sunset *Ideas for Building Barbecues*

Ideas For BUILDING BARBECUES

175 ILLUSTRATIONS
DETAILED PLANS
80 PHOTOS
DIAGRAMS
SKETCHES

$1⁹⁵

Sunset *Ideas for Building Barbecues*, 1950s-1960s. These folks are having a
relaxed, rather proper barbecue, notice the lack of a comical design on the apron.
$8-$10

Bake King Burner Chef Heat Diffuser, metal with wood handle, "Makes a double boiler of every pan in your kitchen," in package, 1950s, Chicago Metallic Mfg. Co., Chicago, IL, Artbeck.

$18-$22

Surface Cooker, "For even-heat cooking an any top-of-the-stove burner, Makes food taste better," in package, 1950s, Arthur Beck Corp., Chicago, IL.

$18-$22

Always be suspicious when a gadget claims to make food taste better.

Oven Shovel, metal, 'The safe, sane way to handle hot pies, cakes, dishes, etc.," boxed, 1950s, Dor-File Mfg. Co., Portland, OR.

$18-$20

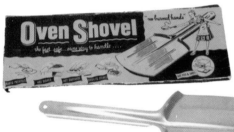

Non-Splash Spatula, stainless steel, "The safe way of turning food in frying pan or griddle," boxed, 1950s, Buckly Culinary Products, Chicago, IL.

$18-$20

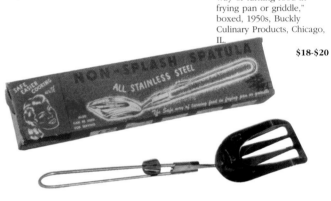

Hi-Speed Safety Kitchen Tongs, metal, "For hot vegetables and other uses, prevents burned fingers," boxed, 1940s, Kitchen Gadget Mfg. Co., Asbury Park, NJ.

$18-$20

Gadget Master Hot Vegetable Tongs, metal, "No more burned fingers, A star in any kitchen," boxed, 1950s, Popiel Bros, Chicago, IL.

$18-$22

Fork and Spoon Combination, highly polished, serves five purposes as shown on backside, boxed, 1950s-1960s, "Made in Japan."

$12-$15

Chapter 17

Corn Gadgets

The popularity of corn, its unique shape, and its many eating and preparation methods have led to a host of products to make preparing and serving it easier. These include numerous servers, holders, butter applicators, and corn-shaped pans for baking. Other products have addressed the need to cut corn off its cob or to cream it. Collectors seek unusual and interesting items, or those that fit in with other kitchen collectibles. Corn's fun image has also resulted in many products having corn-themed graphics, creating great go-alongs for corn lovers.

Life Magazine, July 5, 1937. *Life Magazine's* first year of publication included this feature about July corn on the cover.
$8-$10

Griswold Corn Cake Pan, early American quality cast iron, "There's nothing like iron to cook in," with cardboard sleeve, 1950s, Griswold Mfg. Co., Sidney, OH.

$45-$50

Kristy Korn Kob Pan, cast iron, "Makes delicious, Krunchy, krispy corn bread in a corn cob shape," with cardboard sleeve, 1950s, Wagner Ware.

$25-$30

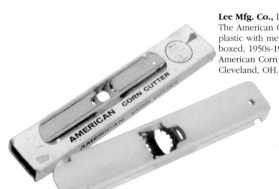

Lee's Corn Cutter, wood with stainless steel blade, 'Cuts both kernel and cream style, No mess, No spatter.' In package 1950s.

$12-$15

Lee Mfg. Co., Dallas, TX. The American Corn Cutter, plastic with metal blade. boxed, 1950s-1960s, American Corn Cutter Co., Cleveland, OH.

$10-$12

Serv-Rite Skewers and Corn Servers, plastic with metal pins, "Authentic cornhusk dishes," in package, 1950s.

$18-$20

Serv-Rite Corn Skewers, with "no drip butter guard," in package, 1950s.

$10-$12

Both from Royal Pacific Co., Los Angeles, CA.

Corn Dishes, set of six aluminum, reusable with skewers, "Corn butters itself, Stays hot longer," in package, 1950s, E-Z-Por Corp., Chicago, IL.

$18-$20

Chef's Corn Cribs, set of six aluminum with paper backing, "For cook-ins, For cook-outs," in package, 1963, Fluted Paper Products Co., S. Norwalk, CT.

$10-$12

"Beauty Bake" Corn Dish ad from *House Furnishing Review*, May 1951.

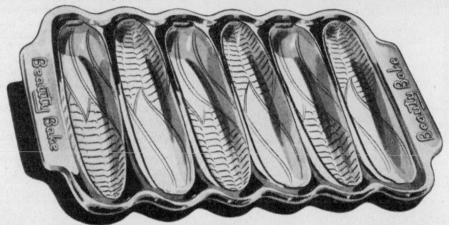

"Beauty Bake" Corn Stick Dish, "Highest quality oven glass for baking or serving," with cardboard sleeve, 1950s, Miracle Maise Mills, Warsaw, IN.

$25-$28

**Serv-Rite Corn Service
Set,** plastic, deluxe 18-piece
set, "The modern way to
serve corn on the cob,"
boxed, 1950s, Serv-Rite
Corn Servers, Los Angeles,
CA.

$25-$30

Smaller sets without butter
dish.

$18-$22

Corn Butter Brush, with
nylon bristles, "No need to
melt butter," on card, 1950s,
W.F. Mayer Co., Yonkers,
NY.

$12-$15

Butter Brush, plastic,
"Spreads butter easily," on
card, 1950s, The Harwood
Co., Farmingdale, NJ.

$12-$15

Harwood's Corn Holders,
plastic with stainless steel
pins, on card, 1950s, The
Harwood Co.

$12-$15

Hot Corn Holders, plastic,
"Sterilize in washing like
fine china," on card, 1950s,
Sanford's, Bellwood, IL.

$10-$12

Corn Butterer, set of four,
stainless steel, boxed,
1960s, Made in Japan,
Viking Importrade,
Moonachie, NJ.

$10-$12

Chapter 18

Egg Gadgets

Eggs are another area of food with its own specialized products and gadgets made to assist in preparation and serving. Whether you wanted to shell it, cook it, separate it, slice it, or even form it into a square, a product was made to aid you. Related items include egg cartons, eggcups, egg timers, etc. Collectors may want to have a few items that appeal to them or concentrate on one area. Eggs and their huge popularity have spawned a mini-industry of their own, and vintage egg-related items continue to increase in popularity.

"The Egg and I" sheet music, 1948, Copyright Universal Pictures Corp.
$8-$12

This country-life comedy introduced film audiences to Ma & Pa Kettle.

Collier's Magazine, April 18, 1936, with cover illustration by Lawson Wood. The rooster seen here seems to be exerting parental control.

$8-$10

"Crax-Ezy" Boiled Egg Opener, plastic, "Stop making like Humpty Dumpty, No more burned fingers," in package, 1950s, M.P. Inc., Los Angeles, CA.

$10-$12

Egg Separator, plastic, "Place it over a cup and break the egg," on card, 1950s, The Harwood Co., Farmingdale, NJ.

$10-$12

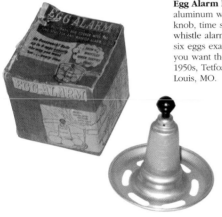

Egg Alarm Egg Cooker, aluminum with plastic knob, time selector and whistle alarm, "Boils up to six eggs exactly the way you want them," boxed, 1950s, Tetfoam Corp., St. Louis, MO.

$18-$22

"Tala" Egg Wedger, metal with wire cutting element, "Slices hard boiled eggs in the nicest way," boxed, 1950s, Taylor Law & Co. Ltd., Stourbridge, England.

$15-$18

Eggwedger, metal, "Cuts hard boiled eggs into 6 uniform sections," boxed, 1950s, Made in W. Germany by Westmark.

$12-$15

Egg Cooking Rack, aluminum, boxed, 1950s, West Bend Aluminum Co., West Bend, WI.

$12-$15

Egg Boiling Rack, aluminum, "Eggs boiled in upright position always have yolks in center," boxed, 1950s, Mullen Crafts Co., Evansville, IN.

$12-$15

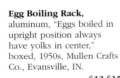

Small-Fry, set of two metal egg cooking frames, "For eggs at their best, Bastes, Fries, Poaches," boxed, 1949, The Benmatt Org., Chicago, Los Angeles.

$12-$15

Egg Cuber, plastic, "Makes a square egg," boxed, 1977, Made in Hong Kong for Aluminum Housewares Co., Maryland Hts., MO.

$8-$10

Egg Timer, plastic, "3 minute," "An absolute kitchen need," in package, 1950s, Del Ray Plastics Corp., New York, NY.

$30-$35

Eggcups, two-part plastic with hand-painted design, 1950s.

$12-$15 pair

"Jiffy Way" Egg Scale, metal with painted scale markings, 1940s, Jiffy Way Inc., Owatonna, MN.

$55-$65

Condition is an important factor with this egg scale, mint boxed examples have sold for over $100 on the Internet.

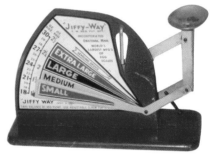

Egg Cartons, Farm Fresh from Old Hickory Smokehouse and One Dozen Eggs, Grade A Medium, 1950s-1960s.

$5-$8 each

Slice Quickly, aluminum, "For vegetables, fruits, eggs," boxed, 1930s.

$15-$18

Deluxe Egg Slicer, plastic and metal, "slices eggs in either direction," on blister card, 1960s, Gemco Products, Hewlett, NY.

$12-$15

Egg Slicer, plastic and metal with red center, 1950s.

$8-$10

Egg Slicer, plastic and metal with round shape, 1950s-1960s, Medco, New York, NY.

$6-$8

Egg Slicer, plastic and metal, 1960s-1970s, Ekco Products Co., Chicago, IL.

$6-$8

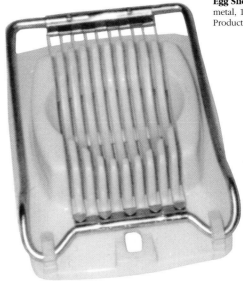

Egg Slicer, aluminum, Lil Cut Up, on blister card, 1960s-1970s, Mirro Aluminum, Manitowoc, WI.

$8-$10

Prestige Sky-line Tomato Slicer, metal with wood handle, "For tomatoes, cucumbers, eggs, etc.," with cardboard sleeve, 1950s.

$15-$18

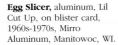

Plasmetl Egg Tray, styrene plastic, 1950s.

$12-$15

Egg Slicer, aluminum, Lil Cut Up, on blister card, 1960s-1970s, Mirro Aluminum, Manitowoc, WI.

$8-$10

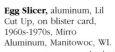

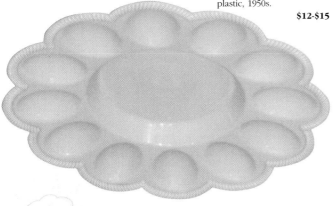

This egg tray, like most Plasmetl products has a fluted edge design.

Chapter 19

Patty Shell Molds, Fry Pan Shields

Patty shell molds are used to deep fry batter into various shapes. A metal form is dipped in batter, deep fried, and the mold is removed to form a crispy batter shell. A typical set includes several differing shapes and a holding rod. A variety of sets were produced over the years as fried batter shells were a common party or luncheon treat. Many patty shell mold sets were kept in their original boxes for storage and to retain enclosed recipes. Collectors search for interesting examples and items having mint-condition boxes.

Saturday Evening Post, April 18, 1953, with cover illustration by John Falter. There isn't much these young cooks haven't experimented with when mom was outside, won't she be surprised!
$8-$10

Griswold Famous Patty Molds, cast iron, 'For tempting, delicious, desserts, salads, etc., boxed, 1950s.

$28-$35

Griswold Mfg. Co., Erie, PA. The Griswold name is well known to collectors who have some of their other cast iron kitchenware, boxes in mint condition bring top dollar.

Griswold Patty Molds, cast iron, boxed, 1950s-60s, Griswold Mfg. Co.

$22-$25

Handi-Hostess Kits. Jumbo Deep Fry Molds or Waffle Plate, Hors D' Oeuvre Molds, cast aluminum with wood handle. boxed, 1950s, Bonley Products Co., Chicago, IL.

$15-$18

 Other varieties of Handy-Hostess kits were made.

8 in 1 Hostess Mold-er-ett, cast aluminum with wood handle, "For Appetizers, Desserts, Hors D' Oeuvres," boxed, 1950s, Bonley Products Co.

$15-$18

"Silver King" Bridge Set, Waf-l-ette Irons, cast aluminum, boxed, 1950s, Silver King Corp., Aurora, IL.

$15-$18

"Silver King" Luncheon Set, Waf-l-ette and Patty Shell Moulds, cast aluminum, 1950s, Silver King Corp.

$15-$18

Nordic-Ware Double Rosette & Timbale Iron, cast aluminum, "Two molds per dip," boxed, 1950s, Northland Aluminum Products Inc., Mnpls, MN.

$15-$18

Nordic-Ware Double Rosette & Timbale Iron, cast aluminum, boxed, 1960s-1970s, Northland Aluminum Products Inc., Mnpls, MN.

$10-$15

French Waffler, aluminum with plastic handles, "French Waffles in a Jiffy, fits right in your toaster!," boxed, 1950s, Fred Stuart Corp., New York, NY.

$18-$22

Patty Shell Set, aluminum, on blister card, 1960s, Made in Japan for Harbor Co., Aurora, IL.

$8-$10

Magic Hostess Spatter-Prufe, aluminum, "Nothing like it anywhere, Lets all the steam out, keeps all the spatter in," in package, 1957, Magic Hostess Corp., Kansas City, MO.

$18-$20

Filter-Fry, aluminum with Bakelite knob, "Takes the spatter out of frying," boxed, 1940s-1950s.

$20-$22

Fry-Pan Cover, aluminum, "No spattering, No mess, No burns," in package, 1950s-1960s, E-Z-Por Corp., Chicago, IL.

$18-$20

Fairgrove Spatter-Prufe, aluminum, "Keeps spatter in, lets steam out," in package, 1971, Made in Japan for Aluminum Housewares Co., Maryland Hts., MO.

$10-$12

Chapter 20

Donut Makers

Donut makers are a simple apparatus for dispensing batter, which became a popular kitchen accessory in the 1950s. The principle involves a spring-activated central plunger, which was held above a fryer to dispense batter in a uniform ring shape. Pancake batter can also be dispensed by the same method, and some of these devices were marketed as pancake makers. Most donut makers were made of aluminum or plastic and have a similar design and operating method. Many companies produced versions, and the plastic ones were offered in varying colors. Examples with their original box are of most interest to collectors. Many packages were saved for their recipes.

Everywoman's, March 1955, with an "infinity" kitchen image on the cover. *Everywoman's* was available at supermarkets in the 1950s for 5 cents a copy.

$6-$8

What a round of pleasure!

CRISCO DOUGHNUTS

(Makes 2½ to 3 dozen)

Fried just right in pure, sweet Crisco, these doughnuts are sure to be delicately sweet and light ... and as *digestible* as they are delicious!

2 eggs	4 teaspoons baking
1 cup sugar	powder
⅓ cup melted	1 teaspoon salt
Crisco	1 teaspoon nutmeg
1 cup milk	Crisco for deep-
4 cups sifted flour	frying

All Measurements Level: Combine beaten eggs, sugar and melted Crisco. Add milk. Mix flour with baking powder, salt and nutmeg. Combine the liquid and dry ingredients, stirring only until smooth.

Roll dough to ½" thickness on a floured board. Dough should be soft. Cut with floured doughnut cutter.

Fry doughnuts in Crisco heated to 365° F. (an inch cube of bread will brown in 60 seconds). Turn when brown and fry on both sides until golden brown (3 to 5 minutes). Remove and drain on paper toweling. If desired, sprinkle with confectioners or granulated sugar before serving.

New lightness! Full flavor! Truly digestible!

What a **difference** when you change from ordinary frying fats to Crisco!

Mmmm! What sweet treats doughnuts *can* be ... so delicately crusted, so fluffy-light! But dollars to doughnuts *you* don't get that kind if you're frying with ordinary fat that has odor and flavor of its own. Such fat tends to *drown out* delicate flavor ... may even give food a *greasy* flavor.

But oh, what a delicious difference when you change to all-vegetable Crisco for frying! It's so pure, so fresh, Crisco lets the delicate good flavor of foods come through while it browns them to perfection. See for yourself how different Crisco is. How white and creamy it looks! How sweet and fresh it smells! And how fresh it *keeps* without refrigeration!

Yes, Crisco lets you enjoy lighter, full-flavored fried foods. And 9 out of 10 *doctors* say Crisco-fried foods are easy to digest. Why, Crisco *itself* is digestible. So for flavor's sake, for *goodness*' sake, start now to fry with Crisco!

fry with
the one and only
Crisco
it's
digestible

THE PROCTER & GAMBLE CO., *makers of Cheer and Joy.*

Crisco Shortening ad with donut recipe from *Good Housekeeping*, April 1952. **$2-$5**

Mirro Donut Maker, anodized gold aluminum, "Easy to use, makes 24 delicious homemade donuts," boxed, 1960s, Mirro Aluminum, Manitowoc, WI.

$15-$18

Mirro Donut Maker Attachment, anodized aluminum, "For use with the Mirro cookie press," on card, 1950s-1960s, Mirro Aluminum.

$10-$12

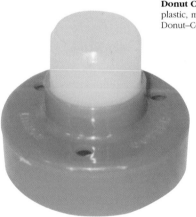

Popeil's Donut Maker, plastic with wooden knob, "Eliminates rolling, cutting, & forming donuts by hand," boxed, 1950s, Popeil Bros, Chicago, IL.

$18-$22

Mirro Donut Cutter, "Also for biscuits and cookies," on blister card 1970s.

$6-$8

Donut Cutter, two pieces, plastic, marked Donut–Cooky Cutter, 1950s.

$5-$7

Minit Chef, Pancaker, plastic with wood knob, "Holds 18, 4" pancakes," boxed, 1962.

$15-$18

Essex Donut Maker, aluminum, "Makes two dozen donuts automatically," boxed, 1950s, Leyse Aluminum Co., Kewaunee, WI.

$18-$20

Maid of Honor Donut Maker, aluminum, "Taste tempting donuts in a jiffy," boxed, 1950s, Sears Roebuck & Co.

$18-$20

Aluminum and plastic donut makers from the 1950s share a common ancestry, some are virtually identical to others except for the company name and box.

Donut Master, aluminum, "Unbreakable, heatproof, fully automatic," boxed, 1950s, either version, DRM Corp., Manitowoc, WI.

$18-$20

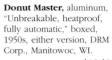

Alumode Donut Maker, aluminum, "The original donut maker," boxed, 1950s, Aluminum Specialty Co., Manitowoc, WI.

$18-$20

"Tala" Doughnut Maker, aluminum with plastic handle ring, "Delicious and so easy to make," boxed, 1950s, Taylor Law & Co. Ltd., Stourbridge, England.

$20-$22

Fairgrove Automatic Donut Maker, aluminum, boxed, 1971, Made in Hong Kong for Aluminum Housewares Co., Maryland Hts., MO.

$8-$12

Chapter 21

Thermometers

Thermometers are another basic kitchen aid with numerous versions produced over the years. The major types include roast meat models having a metal prong to insert into the meat, and glass-enclosed candy or jelly thermometers for inserting into a hot liquid. Other varieties, such as freestanding models for oven use or barbecue grille thermometers, were also made. Vintage thermometers were originally sold separately or in sets. Basic sets would typically include meat and candy thermometers and deluxe sets added basters, skewers, wall racks, etc. Boxed thermometers have the most appeal to collectors today, with colorful box graphics or special features adding interest.

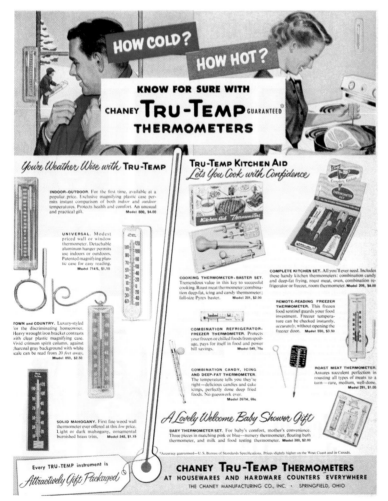

"Tru-Temp" Thermometers ad from *Life Magazine*, November 22, 1954.

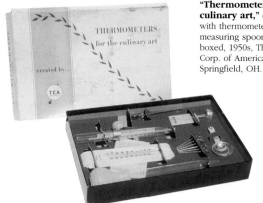

"Thermometers for the culinary art," deluxe set with thermometers, baster, measuring spoons, skewers. boxed, 1950s, Thermometer Corp. of America, Springfield, OH.

$25-$28

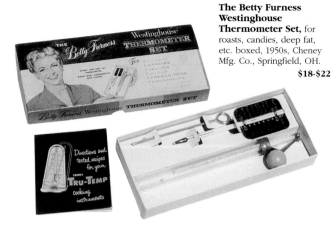

The Betty Furness Westinghouse Thermometer Set, for roasts, candies, deep fat, etc. boxed, 1950s, Cheney Mfg. Co., Springfield, OH.

$18-$22

Ohio Cooking Set, deep fat and meat thermometers, "Measure the degree of your cooking success," boxed, 1950s, Ohio Thermometer Co., Springfield, OH.

$12-$15

Deep Frying Candy and Jelly Thermometer, on blister card, 1960s, John L Chaney Instrument Co., Lake Geneva, WI.

$8-$10

Kitchen Aid Thermometer and Baster Set, boxed, 1950s, The Chaney Mfg. Co., Springfield, OH.

$15-$18

"Tru-Temp" Candy & Deep Fat Cooking Thermometers, "Takes the guesswork out of cooking," boxed, 1950s,Chaney Mfg. Co.

$10-$12

Kitchen Aid Cooking Set, with handy protective wall bracket, boxed, 1950s-1960s, Chaney Tru-Temp div. Of Thermometer Corp. of America, Springfield, OH.

$15-$18

Chef-Master Cooking Thermometer, boxed, 1950s, W.C. Dillon & Co., Chicago, IL.

$12-$15

Maid of Honor Roast Meat & Poultry Thermometer, "For the perfect roast," in cardboard tube, 1950s, Sears Roebuck & Co., made in USA.

$10-$12

Taylor Candy, Jelly, & Deep Frying Thermometer. boxed, 1950s, Taylor Instrument Co., Rochester, NY.

$10-$12

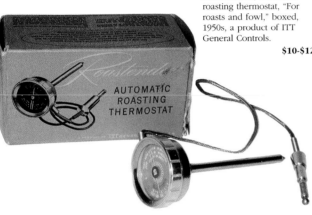
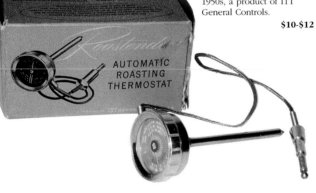

Roastender, automatic roasting thermostat, "For roasts and fowl," boxed, 1950s, a product of ITT General Controls.

$10-$12

Sears Candy, Jelly , Fat Thermometer, in cardboard tube, 1960s, sold by Sears Roebuck & Co.

$10-$12

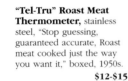

"Tel-Tru" Roast Meat Thermometer, stainless steel, "Stop guessing, guaranteed accurate, Roast meat cooked just the way you want it," boxed, 1950s.

$12-$15

Hostess Meat Thermometer, boxed, 1950s, Langner Mfg. Co., New York, NY.

$8-$10

Meat Thermometer, "No more guesswork," on card, 1950s, Elpo Industries Inc., New York, NY.

$10-$12

Cooper Broil-Well Thermometer, "For all outdoor cooking," on card, 1950s, Cooper Thermometer Co., Pequabuck, CT.

$10-$12

Cooper Cooking Thermometer, stainless steel, unbreakable, "For cooking perfection," on card, 1950s, Cooper Thermometer Co.

$12-$15

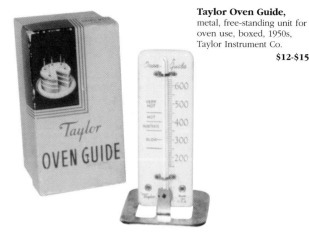

Taylor Oven Guide, metal, free-standing unit for oven use, boxed, 1950s, Taylor Instrument Co.

$12-$15

Roast Meat Thermometer and Double Duty Cooking Thermometer, "The magic wand of a good cook," boxed, 1950s, Ohio Thermometer Co., Springfield, OH.

$12-$15 each

Taylor Candy, Jelly, and Frosting Thermometer, metal and plastic. boxed, 1950s, Taylor Instrument Co.

$12-$15

Taylor Thermometers. Candy, Deep Frying, and Deep Frying Guide, nickel silver plated with wooden handles, boxed, 1950s, Taylor Instrument Co., Rochester, NY.

$18-$22 each

Well-made products and colorful boxes add to collector interest.

Chapter 22

Basters, Roasting Accessories, Potato Bakers, Etc.

According to Julia Child in *The Art of French Cooking*, one of America's great culinary contributions, roasting accessories include products aiding in roast meat preparation. Chief among these are basters used to keep meat moist while roasting. Numerous vintage varieties were produced and original boxes or tube cartons usually include directions for use. Other related items include skewers, heat rods, slicing aids, etc.

A number of vintage products were produced to promote the ease and speed of potato baking. Potato nails were commonly seen gadgets. These metal spikes helped speed up the cooking process through faster heat conduction. Examples on their original packaging card make fun collection additions.

See you at my Tupperware party! This postcard was used as a reminder card for an upcoming party, the lady shown is setting up shop with a Roast Flavor Saver, 1967.

$8-$10

See you at my Tupperware Party!

...just a
reminder of
the day.............
the date.............
the time...........
and the place.....

hostess ....

TUPPERWARE®

... sold only on the home party plan

THP 944-A   Printed in U.S.A.

Lafayette, boasts a restored Standard Oil station not far from downtown.

1958 *Standard Oil Calendar,* from W. Lafayette, Indiana. Crisis in the kitchen, 1950s style, the young lady shown is sobbing when her turkey won't fit in the oven and her husband is pondering their options.

$22-$25

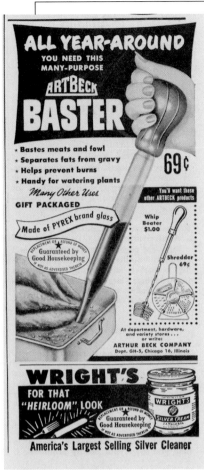

Artbeck Basters, Pyrex glass, with rubber bulb, "An invaluable household aid," unbreakable stainless steel, with rubber bulb and injector, boxed, 1950s, Arthur Beck Co., Chicago, IL, either version.

$18-$22

Ohio Baster, for roast meat and fowl, in cardboard tube, 1950s, Ohio Thermometer Co., Springfield, OH.

$18-$22

Ade-O-Matic, internal and external baster, unbreakable stainless steel, in cardboard tube, 1950s, Ade-O-Matic Co., Chicago, IL.

$18-$22

"Lifetime" Baster, aluminum, "Easy to use, easy to clean," in package, 1950s, made in USA.

$15-$20

Victor Baster, "Kitchen aid," boxed, 1950s, Victor Instrument Mfg. Co., New York, NY.

$18-$22

Ideal Baster, heat proof, "The wonder kitchen utensil," boxed, 1950s, Victor Instrument Mfg. Co., New York, NY.

$18-$22

Baster, unbreakable aluminum with wide opening, in package 1950s, Wecolite Co., New York, NY.

$18-$20

Maid of Honor Basters, Pyrex glass with rubber bulb, "Makes basting easy," with cardboard tube, 1950s either version, sold only by Sears Roebuck & Co.

$18-$22

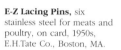

Flavor King Roast Rack, "Assures perfect roasting every time," boxed, 1949, Household Necessities, Chicago, IL.

$10-$12

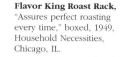

E-Z Lacing Pins, six stainless steel for meats and poultry, on card, 1950s, E.H.Tate Co., Boston, MA.

$8-$10

Turkey Lacers, rustproof, "stuffing is easy," on card, 1950s, The Harwood Co., Farmingdale, NJ.

$10-$12

No Sew Turkey Lacer, stainless steel, "Easy, Quick, Sanitary," on card, 1950s, M.E. Heuck Co., Cincinnati, OH.

$8-$10

Stuffin' Plate, copper-tone aluminum, "No strings, needles, skewers," on card, 1950s, Color Craft, Indianapolis, IN.

$12-$15

Roastand, metal, for oven and grill, "Roasts evenly throughout by scientific method," boxed, 1950s, Domestic Enterprises, Chicago, IL.

$15-$18

Carve-ette by Gerity, chromed metal, boxed, 1950s, Gerity-Michigan Corp., Adrian, MI.

$15-$18

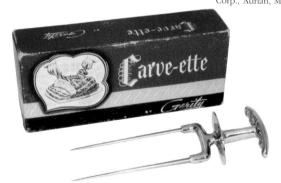

Chef's Pressure Seasoner, boxed, 1950s, Collier Mfg. Co., Oakland, CA.

$12-$15

Foley Roaster, Teflon-finished metal, "With adjustable 'V' rack for full heat circulation," boxed, 1960s, Foley Mfg. Co., Mnpls, MN.

$15-$18

Roasting Pan, metal, "Easy to clean, Completely seamless, Surehold handles," with label, 1950s, Bake King, Chicago Metallic Mfg. Co., Lake Zurich, IL.

$18-$20

Ekco Diathermic Cook Rods, aluminum, "For roasts, chicken, ham, etc., A new idea in cooking, saves 25% of cooking time," boxed, 1950s, Ekco Products Co., Chicago, IL.

$18-$22

Rembrandt Automatic Potato Peeler, plastic with faucet attachment, "Washes and peels automatically, No work, No waste, and unit cleans itself," boxed, 1950s, All Channel Products Corp., Woodside, NY.

$22-$25

Tater Baker, metal with plastic handle, "Bakes potatoes, warms buns and leftovers on top of stove," boxed, 1950, The Everedy Co., Frederick, MD.

$25-$28

"Handi Hostess" Potato Basket and Noodle Nest, "Makes a delicious potato basket for parties, luncheons," boxed, 1951, Bonley Products Co., Chicago, IL.

$18-$22

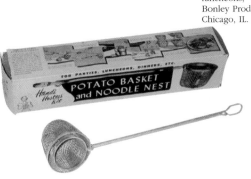

Baking Nails, six jumbo size, aluminum, "Bake potatoes tastier and faster," on card, 1950s-1960s, Wecolite Co., Teaneck, NJ.

$10-$12

Dover, "Potatoe-bake" Rack, "Newest, neatest way to bake potatoes," with insert sheet, 1950s, Dover Products Co., Chicago, IL.

$15-$18

Baking Nails, six, aluminum, "Cooks from inside out, Cuts cooking time 1/3," on card, 1950s-1960s, M.E. Heuck Co., Cincinnati, OH.

$10-$12

Baked Potato Nails, set of six, aluminum, "Now bake fluffier, tastier potatoes faster," on card, 1950s, Nichols Wire & Aluminum Co., Davenport, IA.

$10-$12

Spud Spikes, set of six, aluminum, "Exclusive knife edge, Bake potatoes fast," with card sleeve, 1950s, Monarch Die Casting, Santa Monica, CA

$18-$20

Bake-Rite Potato Bakers, aluminum, "Bakes potatoes evenly in half the time," on card, 1950s, Kewanee rite Products, Kewanee, IL.

$10-$12

Potato Bake Rods, set of four "Thermo-kook" aluminum, "Quick baked potatoes, Fast meat roasting," in package, 1959, A Kenberry Product, John Clark Brown Inc., Belleville, NJ.

$12-$15

Tupperware Roast Flavor Saver Set, 1960s.

$15-$18

I found the inner part of this set by itself, and couldn't quite figure out its intended use. My best guess was a refrigerator watermelon holder!

Chapter 23

Can Openers

Collectors may want to ask what came first, the can or the can opener? It's not hard to reason that a can came first, however, the first can opener, a simple puncturing and cutting device was not far behind. Vintage can openers from the 1930s to 1960s offer collectors a large assortment, varying in design and complexity. Standard types were either handheld or wall mounted, with manufacturers adding extra features, such as a magnetic lid catchers to deluxe models. Prices for the most part remain reasonable, and many collectors search for examples that complement their other kitchen collectibles.

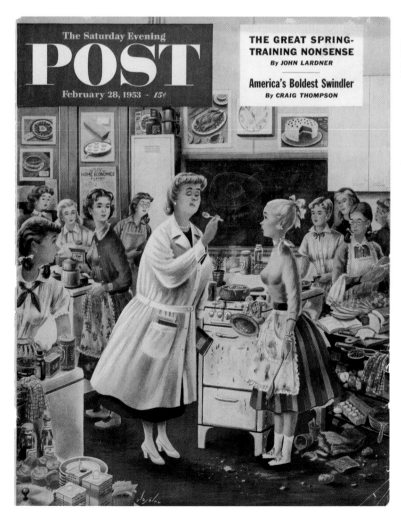

Saturday Evening Post, February 28, 1953, with cover illustration by Constantin Alajalov. A critical moment during home economics class, the instructor taste testing has everyone's full attention. However, the prognosis for the sauce is poor.

$8-$10

Canmaster Can Opener,
chromed metal with
bracket, 1950s.

$8-$10

Can Opener, turquoise
with gold-toned metal,
1950s, Swing-A-Way, St.
Louis, MO.

$8-$12

Can Opener, pink with
chromed metal, 1950s, Maid
of Honor, Sears Roebuck &
Co.

$8-$12

Fint Wall Can Opener,
chromed metal with magnet
lid lifter, boxed, 1950s, Ekco
Products Co., Chicago, IL.

$18-$22

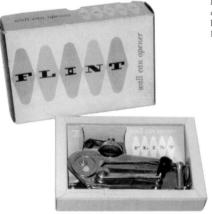

Flint Wall Can Opener,
chromed metal with
bracket, opens square or
round cans, boxed, 1950s,
Ekco Products Co.

$12-$15

**Edlund "Top-Off" Jar
Opener,** metal with wood
handle, "Loosens the
toughest jar caps," 1940s-
1950s, Edlund Co.,
Burlington, VT.

$8-$10

**Edlund "Flat-to-wall" Can
Opener,** metal with wood
handle and built-in magnet,
"Easy to use," boxed, 1950s,
Edlund Co.

$22-$25

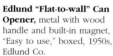

Edlund Jr. Can Opener,
metal with wood handle,
self puncturing, 1940s-
1950s, Edlund Co.

$12-$15

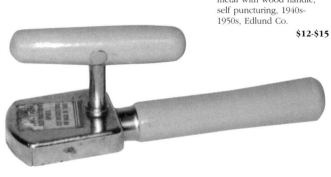

Vaughan's Smoothcut Can Opener, plywood store display, holes in board originally held demonstration unit.

$45-$65

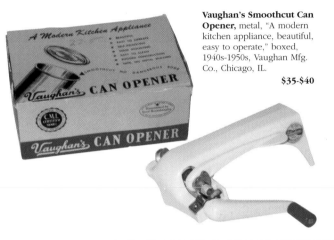

Vaughan's Smoothcut Can Opener, metal, "A modern kitchen appliance, beautiful, easy to operate," boxed, 1940s-1950s, Vaughan Mfg. Co., Chicago, IL.

$35-$40

Flex Roll Wall Can Opener, with magnet attachment, plastic housing with metal, in package, 1950s-1960s, Vaughan Mfg. Co.

$22-$25

Safety Roll Jr. Can Opener, metal, "Opens cans of all sizes, new modern design," on card, 1950s, Vaughan Mfg. Co.

$8-$10 each

Zip Cut Wall Can Opener, metal, "Opens all shaped cans,'" in package, 1950s, Nasco, Japan.

$15-$18

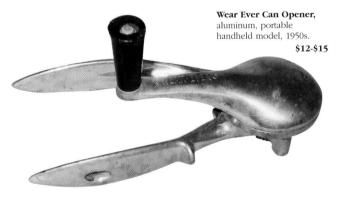

Wear Ever Can Opener, aluminum, portable handheld model, 1950s.

$12-$15

Open cans blindfolded!

Sure you can, because the modern can opener is right there on the wall when you want it, ready to give you finger-tip access to the world's best foods.

It's such a convenient arrangement! Until you're ready to get at those delicious foods with your modern can opener, they're neatly packaged and protected in cans. Billions of these cans yearly are made of dependable-quality tin plate supplied by Jones & Laughlin Steel Corporation.

And the job of getting at innumerable varieties of canned foods is a joy if your can opener wears these words: C.M.I. CERTIFIED MODEL. That's the Can Manufacturers Institute Seal of Approval, given after the can opener has passed rigid tests.

The Seal of Approval assures you that the can opener is safe, smooth-working, grasps the can readily, takes little effort, and it's off with the lid the first time around. It's so easy to use you actually *could* open cans blindfolded if you wished.

You can buy one of the many CERTIFIED models at your nearest department or hardware store. CERTIFIED can openers open cans better.

May 3-8 is National Can Opener Week!

Blue Streak No. A-349-1

Best No. 170

Flint No. 891

Flex Roll Champion

Zim-matic No. Z-12M

Magic Hostess No. 5311

Magna-matic

Dazey No. 88AC

Can-O-Mat No. DL 245

Swing-A-Way No. 1209

Edlund No. 77M

C.M.I. CERTIFIED MODEL

Look for this C.M.I. Seal of Approval on the can opener you buy.

J&L STEEL

Jones & Laughlin
STEEL CORPORATION — *Pittsburgh*

*Look to J & L . . . for the steels
that work for modern industry*

J&L Steel ad featuring can openers from the *Saturday Evening Post,* April 30, 1955. This housewife opening cans blindfolded is so giddy about it, you're sure the men in the white coats can't be too far off! **$2-$5**

Zim Twins Can and Jar Opener, metal with plastic knob, "For opening all food containers," boxed, 1950s, Zim Mfg. Co., Chicago, IL.

$22-$25

Regina Smoothcut Can Opener, "Adjusts to cans of any shape or thickness," boxed, 1940s, Regina Corp., Rahway, NJ.

$18-$20

Deluxe Can Opener, chromed-metal and plastic, on card, 1950s, Vaughan Mfg. Co.

$15-$18

Can Opener, pink metal and chrome, deluxe automatic, with magnetic lid lifter, boxed, 1950s, Swing-A-Way Mfg. Co., St. Louis, MO.

$30-$35

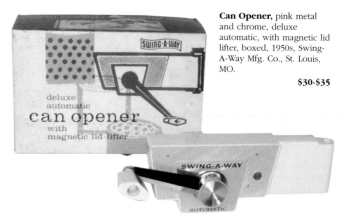

Can Opener, Cabinet Model, "The aristrocrat of can openers, In a gleaming white molded cabinet," 1940s-1950s, Swing-A-Way Mfg. Co.

$30-$35

Can and Bottle Opener, metal with plastic knob, geared, "Swings flat against the wall," boxed, 1940s, Steel Products Mfg. Co.

$15-$18

Wall-Type Can Opener, chromed-metal with plastic knob, with carton, 1940s-1950s, Swing-A-Way Mfg. Co.

$30-$35

Wall Can Opener, metal and plastic, with magnetic lid lifter, boxed, 1960s, Swing-A-Way Mfg. Co.

$15-$18

Swing-A-Way Sales Folder, "For the queen of the kitchen," 1940s-1950s.
$8-$12

Swing-A-Way Can Opener, portable, chrome with plastic-coated handles, boxed, 1950s-1960s, Swing-A-Way Mfg. Co.

$12-$15

Edlund Can Opener Ads from *Good Housekeeping*, November 1951.

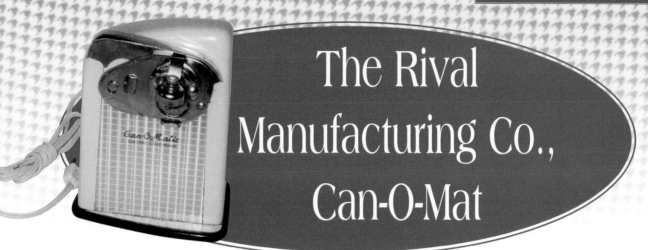

Chapter 24

The Rival Manufacturing Co., Can-O-Mat

The Rival Manufacturing Co. of Kansas City, MO was founded by Henry Talge in 1932. Their first product, the Juice-o-Mat, was shown in early demonstrations to be faster and easier to use than glass reamer-type juicers. It had an early distinction of being available in five different colors, and despite the economy, was widely accepted by consumers. Though its styling was updated on several occasions, its basic lever action stayed the same for many years.

In 1946, Rival introduced a streamlined, hand-cranked, wall can opener, the Can-o-Mat, which was outfitted with a removable cutting wheel in 1949. The Can-o-Mat was available in a range of colors including chrome, and later models had a swinging wall bracket. A number of product additions were made to the line over the years, and included the Ice-o-Mat ice crusher, Knife-o-Mat sharpener, and the Jar-o-Mat jar opener.

In the 1950s, a Trimline Can-o-Mat model was introduced and a company acquisition added the Slice-o-Mat, Shred-o-Mat, and Grind-o-Mat to the line. In 1957, Rival introduced the Can-o-Matic which was one of the first electric can openers, and at about the same time the Ice-o-Matic, a large countertop electric ice crusher, both available in a variety of colors.

In the 1960s, several Rival products were discontinued, including the Juice-o-Mat, which had fallen out of favor with consumers after frozen and packaged juice became widely accepted. In the 1970s, another company acquisition added the popular Rival Crock Pot to the line, and it continues to be successful to the present day.

Today, collectors admire vintage Rival juicers, can openers, ice crushers, and other products for their streamlined Art Deco influenced lines. The variety of colors available adds to their collector appeal. Advanced collectors seek out hard-to-find early models and lesser-known companion products such as the Jar-o-Mat. Pricing can vary considerably. I bought a pink 1950s Rival Can-o-Matic electric opener at a house sale for $4 while the same model and color can sometimes sell for over $60 on the Internet. As with other kitchen collectibles, mint boxed examples and those in red, pink, turquoise, and yellow bring top dollar. In most cases, vintage Rival products were sturdily built and can continue to be used without severely affecting their value.

Can-O-Mat Can Opener,
yellow metal with chromed
handle, deluxe model with
magnet and removable
cutting blade, boxed, 1950s,
Rival Mfg. Co., Kansas City,
MO.

$28-$35

Can-O-Mat Can Opener,
red metal with wall bracket,
boxed, 1950s, Rival Mfg.
Co.

$40-$45

Red color is popular
with collectors.

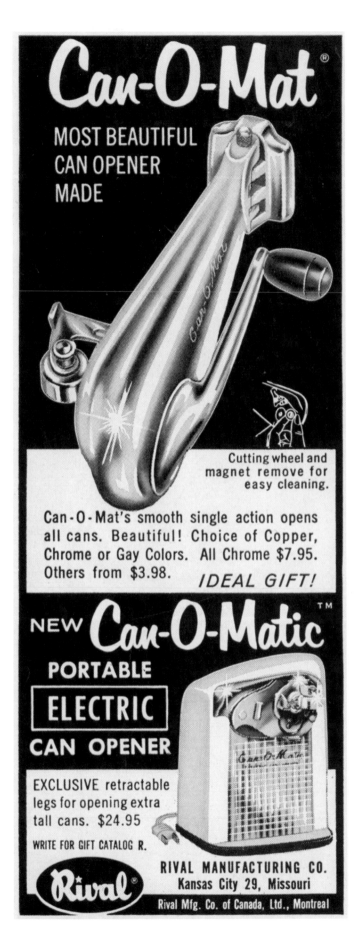

Can-O-Mat ad from *Saturday Evening Post,* June 11, 1960.

Can-O-Mat Can Opener,
all chrome award model
with 24K gold-plated
handle, still sealed in its
can, 1950s, Rival Mfg. Co.
Curious packaging put a
can opener in a can,
thankfully it can be opened
without using a can opener.

$75-$95

Can-O-Mat Can Opener,
turquoise metal with
swinging bracket, 1950s.

$18-$22

Can-O-Mat Can Opener,
chrome metal with swinging
bracket, boxed, 1950s-
1960s, Rival Mfg. Co.

$22-$28

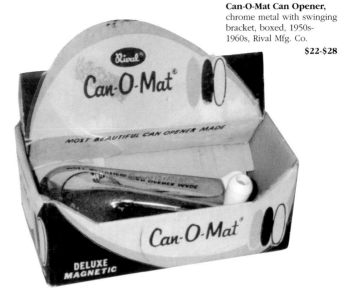

Can-O-Mat Can Opener,
Slimline, pink metal with
chrome, magnetic swing-
type, boxed, 1950s-1960s,
Rival Mfg. Co.

$40-$45

Rival Wall Can Opener,
metal and plastic, "Its
magnetic, It swings," in
package, 1960s, Rival Mfg.
Co.

$18-$20

**Can-O-Matic Electric Can
Opener,** pink metal with
chrome, 1950s-1960s.

$35-$50

Chapter 25

Dazey Corporation

The Dazey Churn and Manufacturing Co. of St. Louis had a thriving business in butter churns starting in the 19th century. Numerous sizes and versions were produced over the years and are now a sought-after collectible. Dazey also produced sharpeners, can openers and other products, and around 1930, they introduced the first wall-mounted can opener. Soon afterward, they acquired the Central States Manufacturing Co. and its Speedo Super Juicer, and introduced the Dazey wall-mounted aluminum juicer.

In later years, improved can openers, sharpeners, eggbeaters, and other products were made, most using the same Dazey wall bracket. In the 1940s an ice crusher, with a modern rocket design plastic ice cup, and plastic juicers were introduced. In 1945, the company was renamed the Dazey Corporation.

The 1950s saw the introduction of boxed gift sets comprised of several of their products, as well as a redesigned ice crusher and a larger deluxe ice crusher set. In 1954, the Dazey Corp. became a subsidiary of Landers Frary & Clark, a large eastern housewares company, known for its Universal brand. Landers Frary & Clark fell on hard times after a series of corporate takeovers and a business downturn, and was acquired by General Electric's housewares division in 1965. The Dazey name was acquired by others and went on to be used on footbaths, the Seal-a-Meal, and other products.

Today, collectors are attracted to the wide assortment of Dazey products. Butter churns are a separate collectible category, and have attracted widespread interest. The early rocket design ice crushers have proven to be a favorite, and are available in painted steel and chrome models with an assortment of plastic cup colors. Ice crushers and ice-cup sets from the 1950s are also popular. Top value for ice crushers is reserved for mint items with bright or pastel colors, while examples in brown, black, or white attract less interest. Companion Dazey products including eggbeaters, juicers, sharpeners, nutcrackers, and can openers all have collector interest.

Canaramic Can Opener,
turquoise metal and
chrome, with magnetic lid
lift, "Complements the
modern kitchen décor,"
boxed, 1950s, Dazey Corp.,
St. Louis, MO.

$25-$30

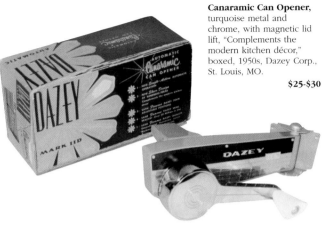

Kwik-Kut Jr. Can Opener,
chromed metal with plastic
handle, "Always handy,
Always ready," boxed,
1950s, Dazey Corp.

$18-$20

Super Senior Can Opener,
white metal with chrome,
boxed, 1950s, Dazey Corp.

$22-$25

Deluxe Can Opener, red
metal with chrome, 1950s,
Dazey Corp.

$18-$22

Juicer, wall mounted,
aluminum with wooden
handle, 1930s-1940s, Dazey
Corp.

$22-$25

Juicer, wall mounted,
aluminum and plastic,
1940s, Dazey Corp.

$22-$25

In the 1940s, plastic
components, like the
reamer and knob
shown on this juicer,
started appearing on
Dazey products.

Ice Crusher, chromed
metal top with black plastic
ice cup, adjusts for fine,
medium, or coarse ice,
boxed, 1940s.

$35-$45

The Early Dazey
Kitchen Helps box is
seldom seen.

Triple Ice Crusher, white
steel top with plastic ice
cup, adjusts for fine,
medium, or coarse ice,
boxed, 1940s-1950s.

$35-$40

Be **Sure** it's a *Dazey*

If you want quality and complete satisfaction — be sure it's a Dazey. The name Dazey has always stood for quality — accept no substitutes. Used with satisfaction in millions of homes throughout the world.

DAZEY CORPORATION • ST. LOUIS 7, MO.

FORM 736   Printed in U.S.A.

DE LUXE

World's finest Can Opener — with greatly improved patented angle cutter. Cuts out entire top of round, square or oval cans . . . smoothly "irons" down rim. Lifts out or swings flat against wall. Model 80 cadmium finish, red knobs. Model 80c chromium finish, trimmed in gay colors.

Dazey 1940s product brochure. In the 1940s, Dazey can openers came in junior, senior, and deluxe models, a range of models similar to automobiles of the era.

$10-$12

Dazey Canaramic ad from *Good Housekeeping*, November 1957.

Ice-Cup-Aid Set, Iceramic crusher and ice bucket, pink metal and plastic with copper tops, adjusts for fine or coarse ice, 1950s, Dazey Corp.

$65-$75

Expect to pay over $100 for mint in box sets.

Ice Crusher, black and chromed steel top with plastic ice cup, adjusts for fine or coarse ice, boxed, 1950s, Dazey Corp., New Britain, CT.

$25-$30

A 1950s restyling gave the ice cup additional capacity, decorator colors add to value.

Super Juicer, wall mounted, two-color plastic, "Be sure to pick a Dazey," boxed, 1940s, Dazey Churn & Mfg. Co.

$40-$45

Also shown is separate counter top mounting unit.

$22-$25

Sharp-It Knife Sharpener, red metal with chrome, 1940s-1950s, Dazey Corp.

$22-$25

Vacumatic Can Opener, red metal and chrome with plastic knobs, 1950s, attached to wall with rubber suction base.

$22-$25

Egg Beater, Blend-R-Mix, stainless steel blades, adjustable handle for right or left-hand use. 1940s, Dazey Corp., metal handle, **$22-$25;** 1950s plastic handle.

$18-$22

Crackit Nut Cracker, metal with wood knob, for use with Dazey wall bracket, boxed, 1950s, Dazey Corp.

$40-$45

Pointz-It Pencil Sharpener, steel and plastic, 1950s, Dazey Corp.

$20-$22

- Whether You're Mixing a Batch of Batter . . . . Opening Cans
- Crushing Ice Cubes . . . Or Sharpening Knives and Scissors
- Dazey Does an Expert, Efficient Job for You

A Egg Beater. Blends, whips or beats! Stainless steel high speed blades designed for easier cleaning. Quiet, smooth-running action; adjustable handle for right or left hand use. Chrome finish with enameled handle and knob in red, yellow or black. **12A $5.95**

DAZEY KITCHEN HELPS . . .

PRACTICAL TO GIVE AND TO OWN

Be sure **it's a** **DAZEY**

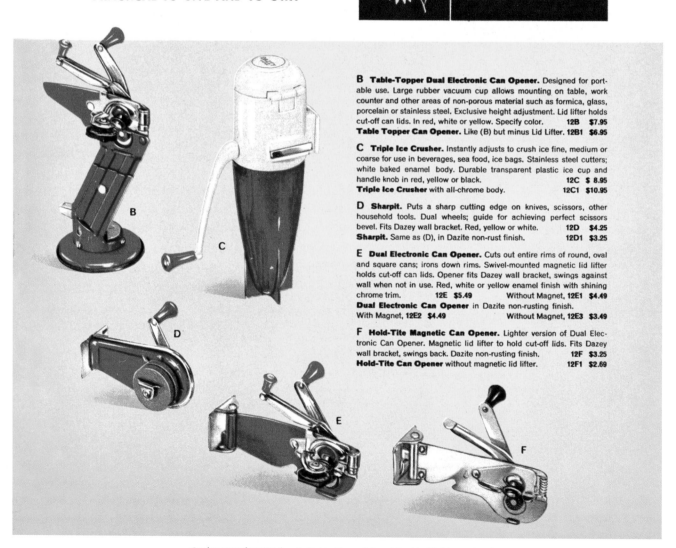

B Table-Topper Dual Electronic Can Opener. Designed for portable use. Large rubber vacuum cup allows mounting on table, work counter and other areas of non-porous material such as formica, glass, porcelain or stainless steel. Exclusive height adjustment. Lid lifter holds cut-off can lids. In red, white or yellow. Specify color. **12B $7.95**
Table Topper Can Opener. Like (B) but minus Lid Lifter. **12B1 $6.95**

C Triple Ice Crusher. Instantly adjusts to crush ice fine, medium or coarse for use in beverages, sea food, ice bags. Stainless steel cutters; white baked enamel body. Durable transparent plastic ice cup and handle knob in red, yellow or black. **12C $ 8.95**
Triple Ice Crusher with all-chrome body. **12C1 $10.95**

D Sharpit. Puts a sharp cutting edge on knives, scissors, other household tools. Dual wheels; guide for achieving perfect scissors bevel. Fits Dazey wall bracket. Red, yellow or white. **12D $4.25**
Sharpit. Same as (D), in Dazite non-rust finish. **12D1 $3.25**

E Dual Electronic Can Opener. Cuts out entire rims of round, oval and square cans; irons down rims. Swivel-mounted magnetic lid lifter holds cut-off can lids. Opener fits Dazey wall bracket, swings against wall when not in use. Red, white or yellow enamel finish with shining chrome trim. **12E $5.49** Without Magnet, **12E1 $4.49**
Dual Electronic Can Opener in Dazite non-rusting finish.
With Magnet, **12E2 $4.49** Without Magnet, **12E3 $3.49**

F Hold-Tite Magnetic Can Opener. Lighter version of Dual Electronic Can Opener. Magnetic lid lifter to hold cut-off lids. Fits Dazey wall bracket, swings back. Dazite non-rusting finish. **12F $3.25**
Hold-Tite Can Opener without magnetic lid lifter. **12F1 $2.69**

Catalog page from Warburg's Variety Store of Grand Rapids, Michigan, showing selection of Dazey products available in the 1950s. Catalog value: **$15-$18**

Chapter 26

Juicers, Ice Crushers

Manual juicers are a throw back to an earlier era. A once frequently seen kitchen gadget, they were made obsolete with the introduction of frozen and canned juice in the 1950s. Most were then relegated to the back of the cupboard. Few people wanted to prepare the fruit and clean up afterwards if all they had to do was open and serve.

Today, most of the interest in juicers is in their novelty. The fact that they are for the most part unnecessary adds to the curiosity factor. However, if someone wants to use a juicer, they seem always ready to be put into service. Collectors enjoy colors to match their decor and find they make interesting bar accessories. Any unusual features, such as integral juice cups, junior sizes, or streamlined styling adds to the appeal.

Ice crushers were a popular party and bar accessory for many years starting in the 1940s. Types varied from handheld units, tabletop models, wall hung, and electrified. Manufacturers offered unique styling features and varied colors to interest consumers. Some units adjusted for coarse, medium, or fine ice, and had separate matching containers.

Today, collectors respond to a favorite color, and matched sets or other special models. Having an original box or other sales materials adds to the value. Many find they are a good compliment to vintage juicers when used as bar accessories.

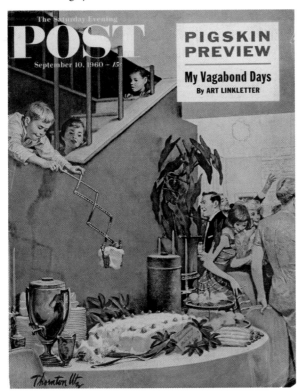

Saturday Evening Post, September 10, 1960. Oops! The kids are trespassing an adults only party with an erector set cake snatcher.

$8-$10

Juice King ad from *House Furnishing Review,* July 10, 1948.

Juice King Whole Orange Juicer, white and chromed metal with plastic handle, "300% faster," 1940s-1950s, National Die Casting Co., Chicago, IL.

$35-$40

Rival Can-O-Mat and Ice-O-Mat ad from *Saturday Evening Post,* April 30, 1955.

Ice-O-Mat Ice Crushers, wall type, metal and chrome top with plastic ice cup, 1950s.

$22-$25

Portable Table Model, metal and chrome top with integral plastic ice cup, 1950s, Rival Mfg. Co., Kansas City, MO.

$25-$30

Juice King Juicers, metal with plastic handle, compact design with removable juice cup, 1940s-1950s, National Die Casting Co.

white   **$22-$25**

red   **$28-$35**

Juicers with minimal paint loss and bright chrome bring the top prices.

Juice King Juicers, metal with plastic handle, compact design with removable juice cup, 1940s-1950s, National Die Casting Co.

$28-$35

Juice-O-Mat, metal with chrome and plastic top, 1940s, full-size unit Rival Mfg. Co., Kansas City, MO $28-$30; junior model.

$25-$28

Juice-O-Mat, metal with chrome top and integral plastic juice cup, 1940s-1950s, Rival Mfg. Co.

$30-$35

Magic Hostess Ice Crusher, metal with chrome top and plastic ice cup, for fine or coarse ice, boxed, 1950s, Magic Hostess Corp., Kansas City, MO.

$25-$30

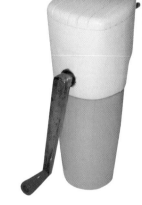

Swing-A-Way Ice Crusher, metal with plastic ice cup, wall mounted, for fine or coarse ice, 1950s, Swing-A-Way Mfg. Co., St. Louis, MO.

$22-$25

Swing-A-Way Ice Crusher, table type, metal and chrome top with plastic ice cup, for fine or coarse ice, 1950s-1960s.

$22-$28

Swing-A-Way Ice Crusher, table type, Lexan plastic, "Portable and convenient," boxed, 1970s, Swing-A-Way Mfg. Co.

$12-$15

The later mostly plastic version lacks sturdiness of earlier models.

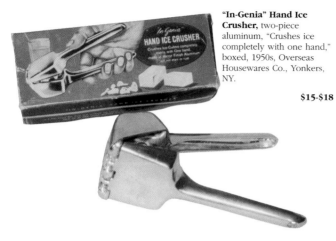

"In-Genia" Hand Ice Crusher, two-piece aluminum, "Crushes ice completely with one hand," boxed, 1950s, Overseas Housewares Co., Yonkers, NY.

$15-$18

Chip Chop Ice Crusher, metal with wood handle, spring and hammer action, "Amazing, Crushes ice cubes right in your glass," boxed, 1950s.

$15-$18

Tap-Icer, metal, "Cracks ice in a jiffy," boxed, 1950s, Tap Icer Co., Williamsport, PA.

$12-$15

Wand-like apparatus allowed users to crack ice in their hand.

"Lightning" Ice Breaker, glass jar with metal ice crushing attachment, crusher "Doesn't hit the glass," in cardboard container, 1940s.

$25-$30

Ice-O-Mat Ice Crusher, portable table model, turquoise and chrome metal with integral plastic ice cup, 1950s, Rival Mfg. Co.

$25-$30

Ice-O-Mat Ice Crusher, portable table model, pink and chrome metal with plastic serving cup base, 1950s.

$28-$35

Ice-O-Mat Ice Crusher, combination table or wall model, white metal and chrome top with plastic ice cup, in-store display package, 1950s-1960s, Rival Mfg. Co.

$35-$45

Ice-O-Matic Ice Crusher, electric countertop model, large metal unit has integral slide out ice cup on the side, made in several colors, 1950s-1960s.

$20-$22

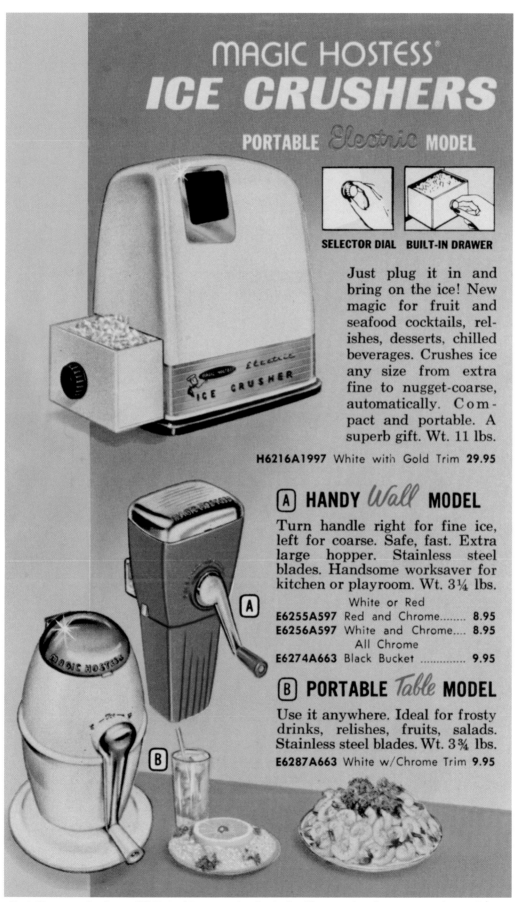

MAGIC HOSTESS®
ICE CRUSHERS

PORTABLE *Electric* MODEL

SELECTOR DIAL   **BUILT-IN DRAWER**

Just plug it in and bring on the ice! New magic for fruit and seafood cocktails, relishes, desserts, chilled beverages. Crushes ice any size from extra fine to nugget-coarse, automatically. Compact and portable. A superb gift. Wt. 11 lbs.

H6216A1997 White with Gold Trim **29.95**

A HANDY *Wall* MODEL

Turn handle right for fine ice, left for coarse. Safe, fast. Extra large hopper. Stainless steel blades. Handsome worksaver for kitchen or playroom. Wt. 3¼ lbs.

White or Red
E6255A597 Red and Chrome........ **8.95**
E6256A597 White and Chrome.... **8.95**
All Chrome
E6274A663 Black Bucket **9.95**

B PORTABLE *Table* MODEL

Use it anywhere. Ideal for frosty drinks, relishes, fruits, salads. Stainless steel blades. Wt. 3¾ lbs.
E6287A663 White w/Chrome Trim **9.95**

Magic Hostess section from a 1959 National-Porges Merchandise Catalog. There must have been some manufacturing synergism between Magic Hostess and the nearby Rival Mfg. Co., their products are virtually identical.

$18-$22

Ice-O-Mat Ice Crusher,
"Bucketeer" table model,
chrome metal top with
plastic serving bucket base,
1950s-1960s, Rival Mfg. Co.

$22-$25

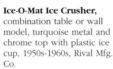

Ice-O-Mat Ice Crusher,
combination table or wall
model, turquoise metal and
chrome top with plastic ice
cup, 1950s-1960s, Rival Mfg.
Co.

$22-$25

Rival Manufacturing Co. ad from *House
Furnishing Review,* July 10, 1948.

Chapter 27

Crank-type Grinders, Salad Makers, Refrigerator Defrosters

Crank-type grinders and salad makers help speed up production when preparing large quantities of food. Heat defrosters were used to combat the mass of ice that would frequently build-up around the freezer compartment of early refrigerators. Boxed versions with interesting graphics or colored aluminum add collector interest.

Magic Hostess Salad Chef and Meat Grinder page from a 1959 National-Porges merchandise catalog. Catalog value: **$18-$22**

Chrome grinder models were premium priced when new.

Magic Hostess Meat Grinder and Salad Chef, chromed metal with attachments, boxed, 1950s, Magic Hostess Corp., Kansas City, MO.

$22-$25

Saladeer Salad Maker, chromed metal, deluxe three cone with patented cone-grip lock, boxed, 1950s, Rival Mfg. Co., Kansas City, MO.

$20-$25

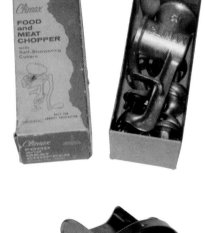

Climax Food and Meat Chopper, metal, with self sharpening cutters, boxed, 1950s, Universal, Landers Frary & Clark, New Britain, CT.

$18-$22

Grind-O-Mat Meat Grinder and Food Chopper, chromed metal with attachments, boxed 1960s, Rival Mfg. Co.

$20-$25

Shred-O-Mat Food Slicer, yellow metal with chrome top, attachments, and wooden handle, 1950s, Rival Mfg. Co.

$28-$35

This food shredder is available in kitchen coordinating colors.

Kitcheneer, white metal with chrome top, the Kitcheneer set included a Grind-O-Mat shown and a Shred-O-Mat with one mounting stand, 1950s, Rival Mfg. Co.

$35-$40

Coffee-Mill, red metal and chrome top with clear plastic container and wooden handle, wall mounted, "There's nothing like freshly ground coffee for full-bodied flavor in every cup," boxed, 1950s, Rival Mfg. Co.

$50-$65

Seldom seen Rival gadget in red appeals to collectors.

Grind-O-Mat, coral metal base with chrome top and wooden handle, 1950s, Rival Mfg. Co.

$35-$45

This early grinder model shows the degree of quality these units had before cost-saving designs were implemented.

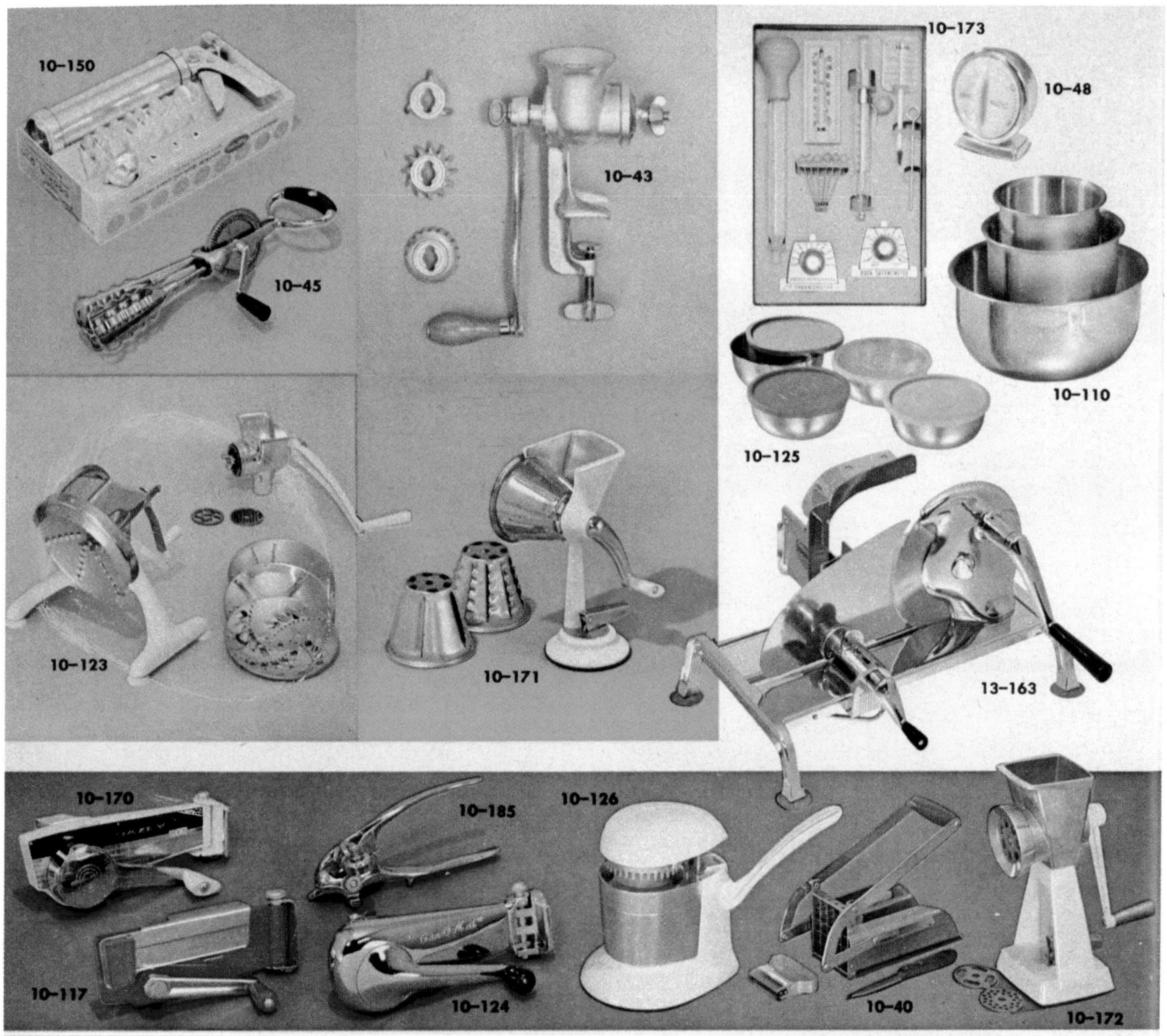

WONDER-WORKING COOKING AIDS SAVE YOU TIME

FREE FOR FAMOUS TOP VALUE STAMPS

10–40 French Fry Cutter by Burns. With potato peeler and paring knife. Nickel plated for rustproof beauty.................1 book

10–43 Universal Food Chopper. Self sharpening. 3 cutters–coarse, medium or fine. Clamps securely to table..............1⅖ books

10–45 Flint Best Egg-Beater. For faster, easier mixing—8 stainless steel scalloped shaped blades. Nylon gears..........1⅕ books

10–48 Mirro-Matic Timer. For pressure cooker timing, percolating or baking. Requires no winding; just set dial and bell rings when time is up. Chrome-plated...............1⅕ books

10–110 Vollrath 3-Pc. Mixing Bowl Set. Unbreakable stainless steel lasts a lifetime. Includes ¾ qt., 1½ qt., 3 qt. bowls..1⅖ books

10–117 Swing-A-Way Magnetic Can Opener. Magnetic lid-lifter picks up and holds lid. Swings back out of the way. White, red, yellow.................1 book

10–123 Rival "Kitcheneer." Combination food grinder-chopper, shredder, slicer, grater. Converts from meat grinder to salad maker. Lightweight, portable, needs no clamps. White only.... ....4 books

10–124 Rival All-Chrome Magnetic Can-O-Mat. 3-position wall bracket..............2⅕ books

10–125 Olympic Stainless Steel Food Saver Set. Four 1 pint bowls with air-sealed lids. Ideal for refrigerator..........1 book

10-126 Rival Juice-O-Mat. Juices 6 oranges in 90 seconds. Top tilts automatically. White enamel base and top; removable aluminum pitcher.....2⅘ books

10–150 Wear-Ever Cookie Gun Pastry Decorator. Equipped with automatic control to dial desired thickness. 9 cookie shapes, 3 pastry tips. Recipe book included. ....1⅖ books

10–170 Dazey Magnetic Can Opener. Opens all sizes and shapes. White baked enamel; chrome trim...........2 books

10–171 Dazey Salad Maker. Three cones for slicing, shredding and grating. 4″ sure-grip vacuum base. White baked enamel with chrome trim............3 books

10–172 Dazey Food and Meat Chopper. Complete with four cutters. Vacuum sure-grip base, non-rust aluminum hopper, white aluminum base.......2⅘ books

10–173 Kitchen Thermometer Set. Nylon baster, candy thermometer, roast meat thermometer, oven thermometer, refrigerator thermometer and six lacing skewers....................1 book

10–185 Rival Magnetic Hand Can-O-Mat. Chrome finish, lightweight die cast aluminum. Opens all cans................1 book

13–163 Rival "Protect-O-Matic Food Slicer. All Chrome finish. 6½″ serrated blade slices any food..................5 books

Page 60

Special Order items—see page 97

Page from a Top Value Stamps catalog showing a Shred-O-Mat, Grinder, and other 1950s kitchen gadgets. Many of these items were made of durable metals, and with care can continue to be used by collectors without severely affecting their value. Catalog value: **$15-$18**

Heatflo Defroster, electric, for refrigerator and freezer, metal, "For fast, clean, defrosting," boxed, 1950s, Chromalox, Murfreesboro, TN.

$22-$25

Ostrow 700 Defroster, infrared, metal with plastic handle, thermostat controlled, "Defrosting's a breeze," boxed, 1950s.

$20-$25

Electra Frostaway, for refrigerator and freezer, copper-toned metal with wooden handle, "Fast, Easy, Safe, Frozen foods have no time to thaw," boxed, 1950s.

$28-$35

Defrost King, plastic and metal defrost timer, "Set it, Forget it," boxed, 1950s, Galter Products Co.

$18-$22

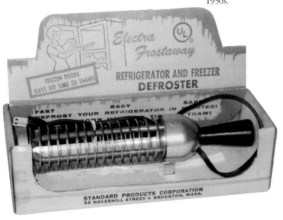

Davis Defroster, infra-red, for refrigerator and freezer, metal with plastic handle, "Works so fast that frozen foods can't thaw," boxed, 1950s, Davis Mfg. Co., Plano, IL.

$22-$25

Bel-Air Super Defroster, 500 watt infra-red, color-toned aluminum with wooden handle, "Defrosts refrigerators and freezers without muss or fuss," boxed, 1950s, Bel-Air Appliances, Lynwood, CA.

$22-$25

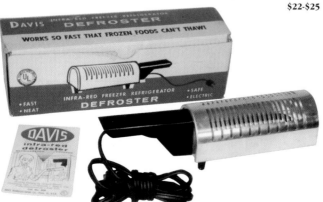

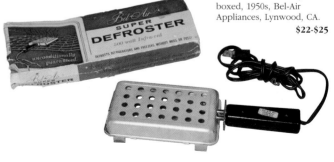

Chapter 28

Gadgets as Giveaways

The history of getting something free with a purchase goes back to ancient times. In the 1800s, figural candy containers and other products provided an extra sales incentive for customers. When Nabisco first started selling crackers in their own package, during the early 1900s, the package itself was a sales incentive. It was a handy easy-to-use way of carrying the product and assuring that it would stay fresh until use. In the years to come, the idea of a package having a purpose would become more fully developed, as well as the notion of adding a "free" item inside the package as an extra sales incentive.

Early product giveaway promotions from the 1920s to the 1940s enabled buyers to get a free added product, such as a dish or a towel with their cereal or detergent purchase. This encouraged repeat purchases, as the buyer likely wanted additional dishes or towels to match the first one. Cereal companies such as Quaker Oats and detergent brands including Breeze, Duz, and Silver Dust had successful long-running promotions of this type.

Other companies and product packages helped develop the idea that the container could be shaped into a useful, reusable item such as a glass, server, canister, etc. Jelly and peanut butter was successfully promoted by giving the buyer a decorative glass or serving piece. Swift & Co. successfully sold peanut butter in colorful glasses featuring the Wizard of Oz characters and other designs. Big Top peanut butter was sold in containers that could double as serving pieces. Welch's jelly, Kraft, Natco, and others had similar success with their own offerings in this area. Numerous different items have been produced over the years.

Coffee and syrup companies took this notion further by packing their product in reusable servers or decanters, usually on a special limited-time basis. Companies and brands included General Foods, Sanka, Log Cabin, and others. Nescafe coffee even came packaged in a Skotch picnic jug for a time in the 1950s. Purity Oats as well as Fluffo and Crisco shortening were sold in colorful decorative cans, which could be reused when empty as canisters for flour, sugar, etc.

Reusable packaging promotions continue to this day, and older examples continue to attract collector attention. Presently, glasses with colorful patterns or character designs have become a popular collecting category on their own.

Some companies offered gadgets having a colorful product character incorporated into the design that a customer could send away for at a modest cost. Aunt Jemima pancake mix offered a series of these items featuring the popular images of Aunt Jemima and Uncle Moses. Products offered included shakers, spice containers, syrup servers, cookie jars, etc. Aunt Jemima cake mixes, in one of their less well-known product offerings, gave away colorful plastic spoons and candleholders. These were packaged inside the box like a Cracker Jack toy in the early 1950s, and are seldom seen today. Another company having success with promotional send away for items was Planters. Over the years, Planters has issued banks, mugs, pens, shakers, dishes, nut choppers, etc., all featuring the ever-popular, Mr. Peanut.

Numerous other companies have had success offering bowls, mugs, shakers, etc. over the years. These include Kelloggs, Ovaltine, Pillsbury, Nestles, Campbells, Bordens, etc. Older items featuring colorful characters or graphics continue to increase in popularity. Good luck trying to find one of these pieces at a price as reasonable as the one the original buyer paid!

Silverware and cutlery were popular premiums for many years, available with the payment of coupons and/or a modest price. General Mills had success with a long running promotion of Queen Bess silverware in the 1950s where coupons were included inside every product they made. Adding a small amount of money greatly reduced the number of coupons needed to get silverware. All Sweet margarine from Swift & Co. had a similar silverware promotion.

Other companies and products including Lipton Soups, Old Dutch Cleanser, Swiftning Shortening, Mazola Oil, Campbells, etc. offered turkey baster sets, knives, glasses, pans, cutlery, shears, cleavers, even live plants! The list goes on and on. The variety of items is extensive and are increasingly attracting collector attention. Perhaps the ultimate giveaway was when Playtex gloves gave out a free right hand in every box!

"Silver Flake" Chinaware Oats Box, originally a piece of chinaware was packaged along with the oats, 1920s-1930s, Great Northern Illinois Cereal Co.

$28-$35

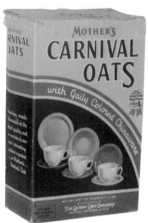

Mother's Carnival Oats Box, "With gaily colored chinaware," 1930s-1940s, The Quaker Oats Co., Chicago, IL.

$35-$45

Unmarked China was from Homer Laughlin with colors similar to those available on Fiesta dinnerware.

$8-$15 each

Quaker Oats Box, with mail-in promotion for hand-painted "Apple Pattern" China Ware, 1950s, The Quaker Oats Co.

$25-$35

Apple Pattern China Ware, was made by Blue Ridge, cup and saucer.

$22-$28

Duz Detergent Box, with dinnerware inside, sealed, 1950s-1960s, Proctor & Gamble.

$75-$85

One piece of Golden Wheat pattern china was included with detergent, matching service pieces could be ordered separately; cup and saucer with box $18-$22; plate with box, glass with box, or gravy boat.

$12-$15

Serving pieces are scarcer because they were available by mail

Silver Dust Detergent Box, giant size with "Silver Leaf" Libbey glass inside, 1960s. On the backside you could "Set a lovely table with elegant satin-etch matching pieces."

$25-$30

Lever Brothers Glass with box.

$12-$15

Sugar and creamer set.

$25-$28

32 oz. Hostess pitcher.

$28-$35

Silver Dust Detergent Box, regular size with "Silver Leaf" Libbey juice glass inside, sealed 1960s, Lever Brothers.

$35-$40

Silver Dust Detergent Box, regular size with fine Cannon face cloth inside, sealed, 1950s, Lever Brothers.

$25-$30

Ivory Snow Detergent Box, giant size with free toy inside, 1960s.

$25-$28

Proctor & Gamble, plastic baby toy.

$15-$18

Vel Detergent Box, with free Scotch brand tape and dispenser inside, 1950s.

$25-$28

Metal Scotch Tape Dispenser.

$8-$10

Cheer Detergent, giant size with two plastic tumblers inside, 1950s-1960s, Proctor & Gamble

$25-$28

Add $10-$12 if tumblers are present. Box mentioned that you got the full measure of detergent as well as the promotion.

Oxydol Detergent, king size with a set of three wooden spoons inside, 1950s.

$25-$30

Add $10-$12 if spoons are present.

$100,000.00 "It's a BREEZE" CONTEST!
ALL-PURPOSE DETERGENT

Win Your Height In Dollars!

Just for completing this sentence: *"I like the lovely Cannon premiums in Breeze all-purpose detergent because..."*

1st PRIZE your height in dollars— guaranteed minimum ... **$18,000.00**

2nd PRIZE **$10,000.00**

3rd PRIZE **$5,000.00**

FIVE 4th PRIZES ... **$1,000.00** Each

PLUS 1175 Westinghouse PRIZES

25 REFRIGERATOR-FREEZERS
New cold injector, Frost-Free model, with separate freezer. Keeps meats fresh 7 days without freezing.

50 MOBILAIRE® AIR CONDITIONERS
New one-ton air conditioner for complete summer comfort. Easily movable from room to room.

100 CLOTHES DRYERS
New electric model has 4 drying temperatures. One for wash-n-wear. Direct air flow system dries faster.

1000 COFFEE MAKERS
New spoutless model. Ends cleaning problems. Makes fresher, more delicious coffee every time.

Just imagine! No matter how tall, you stand to win $286 per inch. And no matter how small, there's a guaranteed minimum of $18,000 first prize money! And remember, Breeze is the finest all-purpose detergent your money can buy!

It's a breeze to enter—a breeze to win! Just tell us why you like the lovely Cannon premiums you get at no extra cost with Breeze! There's a Cannon bath towel in King size, a Cannon kitchen towel in Giant size, a Cannon face cloth in Regular size.

NOTE: First prize computed on basis of 286 crisp, new $1 bills per inch of height—$18,000 guaranteed minimum!

CONTEST RULES:1. In fifteen additional words or less, complete the statement: "I like the lovely Cannon premiums in Breeze all-purpose detergent because..." Here's a sample entry, "I get face cloths, kitchen towels and bath towels—all as an *extra!*" Use entry blank at right (also available at many grocers) or your own paper. Send as many entries as you wish to: Breeze Contest, P. O. Box 41B, Mount Vernon 10, New York.

2. With each entry send a box-top from Breeze, any size. Entries must be postmarked not later than July 15, 1959 and received by the judges by July 22, 1959. Affix adequate postage. No entries returned. All become property of Lever Brothers Company.

3. Entries will be judged by the staff of The Reuben H. Donnelley Corporation for originality, sincerity and aptness of thought. Judges' decisions are final. Duplicate prizes awarded in case of ties. Only one prize to a family. Prizes are listed elsewhere on this page.

4. Everyone in the United States may enter except employees of Lever Brothers Company, its subsidiaries, its advertising agencies ... and members of their immediate families. Entries must be original work of contestant submitted in own name. Contest subject to federal, state, and local regulations.

5. Winners will be notified by mail approximately six weeks after contest closes. Send stamped self-addressed envelope for list of winners if desired (available six weeks later).

BREEZE CONTEST, P. O. Box 41B, Mount Vernon 10, New York

"I like the lovely Cannon premiums in Breeze all-purpose detergent because_____

_____

_____"

(complete in fifteen additional words or less)

Name_____

Street & Number_____

City_____Zone_____State_____

Mail by July 15, 1959. Include Breeze boxtop. Use adequate postage.

Breeze Detergent ad, with free towels and "It's a Breeze" contest. *Good Housekeeping,* June 1959.

$2-$5

Breeze Detergent Box, giant size with Cannon dishtowel inside, sealed, 1950s, Lever Brothers.

$30-$35

If the free towel didn't appeal to you, the "Special offer electric wood warmer for $1" might seal the purchase.

Breeze Detergent Box, two-tone stripe Cannon face cloth inside, sealed, 1960s $22-$28; with pastel Cannon face cloth inside, sealed, 1950s $25-$30; giant size with Cannon bath towel inside 1960s $25-$30;. towel premium with box, Lever Brothers.

$15-$18

Consumers eventually realized that towels displaced a good portion of the contents, and lost interest when towels were not needed.

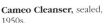

All Detergent Box, with "60 Valiant Contest," sealed, 1960, Lever Brothers.

$30-$35

The contest graphics and prize pictures dominate this detergent box.

Cameo Cleanser, sealed, 1950s.

$22-$25

Cameo Cleanser Holder, two-piece plastic with attached cameo, 1950s.

$18-$22

Get this exclusive "Early American" Glassware every time you buy BIG TOP Peanut Butter

LOOK! New glamour for your table!

The PEANUT BUTTER with the fresh-roasted flavor of peanuts at the circus!

Big Top's Roto-roasting—that's the secret that brings out all the golden goodness of the peanuts . . . gives Big Top Peanut Butter its delicious fresh-roasted flavor. Whip-blending makes it so creamy, too, for easy spreading. Yes, Big Top really tastes as tempting as it looks in these lovely crystal-clear goblets and sherbets. Treat your family to Big Top and start collecting this "Early American" stemware to sparkle on your table!

Big Top is another great food product from Procter & Gamble

Also comes in handy Refrigerator Jars

BIG TOP PEANUT BUTTER

Copr. W. T. Young Foods, Inc., subsidiary of The Procter & Gamble Company

AT YOUR STORE NOW, OR COMING SOON!

Big Top Peanut Butter ad featuring, "Early American" glassware, from *Ladies Home Journal*, February 1957.

$2-$5

Big Top Peanut Butter, W.T. Young Foods, div of Proctor Gamble, sealed large water goblet $30-$35; small dessert dish with lid.

$15-$20

Old Dutch Cleanser ad with kitchen shears offer, *Woman's Day*, September 1950.

$2-$5

Cleanser cans with unusual names or graphics are more collectible.

Dutch Cleanser Can, sealed, 1950s.

$18-$22

Kitchen Shears, similar to those in ad.

$8-$12

GREASE REMOVED 7 TIMES FASTER
SUDSING ACTION 11 TIMES GREATER

No Wonder Famous OLD DUTCH CLEANSER Made with Activated Seismotite *(PATENTED PROCESS)* cleans with

Twice the Speed

of the average of ALL other leading cleansers

You'll call Old Dutch a true wonder worker! Amazing new grease-dissolver cuts grease on contact! Rich suds, filled with Activated Seismotite, float away grease, grime, dirt faster than ever before. Even greasiest roasters, pots, pans and porcelain come gleaming clean! Safe! You'll like Old Dutch's speed . . . you'll like its fresh, clean, pleasant fragrance, too. Try famous Old Dutch—the only cleanser made with Activated Seismotite.

Here's the Proof From Scientific Laboratories!

CLEANSER	CLEANING EFFICIENCY
OLD DUTCH	100%
CLEANSER A	58.3%
CLEANSER B	50.0%
CLEANSER C	48.5%
CLEANSER D	42.5%

Average 49.8%

BACK AGAIN **KITCHEN QUALITY SHEARS**
$2.25 Value—Yours for Only

MAIL THIS COUPON NOW to
Old Dutch Cleanser, Dept. 1
Box U, Chicago 77, Illinois

$1.00 and Windmill Pictures from 2 Old Dutch labels

AMAZINGLY STRONG! EXTRA SHARP! HIGHEST QUALITY CUTLERY STEEL.

Like Old Dutch, these handy Kitchen Shears make quick work of "toughest" jobs! They cut up chicken, dice vegetables, scale fish. Crack nuts, on-cap bottles, pry off lids. Trim shrubs, cut flowers. Sanitary! Come apart for easy cleaning. Sharp, sturdy! Actual size 8½ inches long.

Bargain Offer
TO INTRODUCE YOU TO NEW
"EXTRA-DUTY" DUZ!

Never before such White Washes with so much Color Safety!

You mustn't miss new Duz with Extra-Duty Formula! It turns out the *whitest* Duz washes ever—and with *greater safety for colors* than any other leading washday package soap!

No soap on earth gets clothes *cleaner* than this new "Extra-Duty" Duz! Yet this same soap that gives your towels and sheets the most marvelous new whiteness and chases deepest-down dirt out of the grimiest overalls is actually *safest for colors!* Yes, it's safer than any other "bigname" washday package soap for *all* your colored washables!

Get "Extra-Duty" Duz today—take advantage of this money-saving offer right away!

DUZ does EVERYTHING

$1⁵⁰ Value
SLICING KNIFE
ONLY **50¢**
with 2 DUZ box-tops

12½" KNIFE!
8" BLADE!
Big all-purpose knife with hollow-ground, scalloped blade. Won't rust, stain, tarnish. Red Tenite plastic handle is molded on—won't loosen or come off!

NEW MIRACLE BLADE
stays sharp far longer!

Made by sensational new process! Unlike ordinary stainless steel knives, this new "Quikut" hollow-ground blade stays keen and sharp far longer!

It's the latest, greatest improvement in stainless steel cutlery—and now Duz brings

it to you at only a fraction of its actual retail value!

You'll want this big, easy-cutting knife to make quick work of dozens of kitchen jobs. So go to your grocer right away —send for as many as you want while this bargain offer lasts!

Here's How to Get it!

Look for this 2-Package Special at your dealer's! You get 2 boxes of new "Extra-Duty" Duz with complete details of knife offer and HANDY ORDER BLANK! If your dealer doesn't have this 2-package special, send 50¢ in coin (no stamps, please) with 2 Duz box-tops and your name and address plainly printed to: DUZ, Box 111, Cincinnati 1, Ohio.

Offer good in Continental U. S. and Hawaii—expires July 31, 1950.

MARCH, 1950   23

Duz Detergent ad, with slicing knife offer, *Woman's Day,* March 1950.
$2-$5

Duz Detergent Box, "Duz does everything!," sealed, 1950s, Proctor & Gamble.
$22-$25

Quikut Slicing Knife with plastic handle, 1950s.
$8-$12

Aunt Jemima Cake Mix ad, with candleholders offer, *Woman's Day,* December 1951.
$5-$7

Aunt Jemima Candle Holders, plastic, 12 different fairy tale designs, F&F Die Works, Dayton, OH, set of six.
$30-$35

Add $25-$30 if small shipping box with Aunt Jemima picture is included.

Aunt Jemima Pancake Box, sealed, 1960s.
$45-$65

Aunt Jemima Magical Recipes Booklet, 1950s.
$22-$25

Androck Syrup Server, plastic handle, 1930s-1940s.
$35-$40

Aunt Jemima and Uncle Moses Salt and Pepper Shakers, plastic 3-1/2" high, marked F&F Die Works, Dayton, OH, 1950s.
$55-$75

With Aunt Jemima figures, paint condition and wear affect value.

Get Your Gay
Mother Goose
Candle Holders!

FREE OF ADDED COST!

ONE INSIDE EVERY SPECIALLY MARKED PACKAGE OF
Aunt Jemima CAKE MIXES

No box tops! No waiting! You'll find a gay Mother Goose Candle Holder inside every specially marked package of Aunt Jemima Silver Cake and Devil's Food Mix.

Get Little Bo-Peep, the Cat and the Fiddle, King Cole—12 different figures in all! Sparkling washable plastic. Offer limited—don't delay. Get Aunt Jemima Cake Mixes today!

...Get Real
Homemade Goodness!

Only My Cake Mixes Give You Such Homemade LIGHTNESS!.. TEXTURE!..FLAVOR!

...and **NOTHING TO ADD**— Country-Good Eggs and Milk Already in!

Aunt Jemima CAKE MIXES
Silver Cake and Devil's Food

SILVER CAKE / DEVIL'S FOOD CAKE

Look for these Special "Candle Holder" Packages!

98

Babbitts or Bab-O Cleanser Cans, 1950.

$22-$25

Aunt Polly's Decorator Set, a Babbitt mail in offer, boxed, 1950s.

$20-$22

Welch's Grape Juice Bottle, with Howdy Doody label, 1950s.

$35-$40

Swift's Peanut Butter Wizard of Oz Glasses, 1950s.

$18-$22 each

Ann Page Peanut Butter Glass, with label, 1950s.

$15-$18

Welch's Grape Jelly Glass, with character design and label, 1950s-1960s.

$18-$20

Aunt Jemima Pancakes ad, with salt and pepper shakers offer, *Woman's Day,* April 1951.

$5-$7

Kraft Cream Cheese in Pyrex Baking Cup, with plastic lid, 1960s.

$10-$12

National's Orchard Fresh Apple-Raspberry Jelly Glass, with printed design and label, sealed 1950s-1960s.

$22-$25

Sanka Coffee, special low-priced coffeemaker, heatproof glass with plastic handle and metal collar, sealed with label, 1960s-1970s.

$22-$25

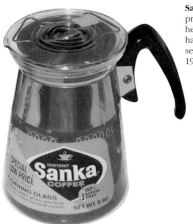

Maxwell House Coffee, Free Carafe, heatproof glass with plastic handle and metal collar, with label, 1960s.

$20-$22

Log Cabin Syrup, free pitcher, decorated glass body and plastic top, with label, 1960s-1970s.

$15-$18

Nescafe, special low-priced Skotch Jug, insulated metal and plastic top, with label 1950s.

$22-$28

Fluffy Shortening, free canister, metal with printed design, sealed with label, 1950s, Proctor & Gamble.

$25-$28

Fluffy Shortening, Shortening canister, with printed design and plastic lid, 1950s-1960s.

$8-$10

Aunt Jemima Spoons, plastic, fairy tale designs, F&F Die Works, Dayton, OH.

$6-$8 each

Purity Oats, free canister, metal with apple design, with label 1950s, General Mills.

$25-$28

Thomas J. Webb Coffee Can, 1950s.

$10-$15

Thomas J. Webb Promotional Tongs, originally available for 10 cents and can coupon, boxed, 1950s.

$12-$15

Carnation Shaker, two-piece metal with "Carnation" embossed on lid, 1950s.

$15-$18

Quaker Oats Pitcher-Mugs, Quaker, painted plastic, 1940s-1950s.

$20-$25

Roy Rogers, painted plastic, 1950s.

$35-$40

Carnation Malted Milk Chocolate Flavor, with contents and label, 1950s.

$20-$22

Ovaltine Shake-Up Mug, with Little Orphan Annie decal, two-piece beetleware plastic, "Cold Ovaltine" embossed on lid, 1930s-1940s.

$35-$50

Condition of plastic and decal is critical on these Ovaltine radio promotion items.

Cup, with Little Orphan Annie decal, plastic, 1930s-1940s.

$25-$28

Try all three...

The famous two... plus one that's new

NEW!

NEW DELUXE
Buttermilk
PANCAKE
MIX for waffles, too!

Get this shaker Free!

Makes perfect pancakes in 10 shakes!
It's so easy to make 'em when you *shake* 'em! Just pour in the ingredients, shake ten times, and pour out perfect pancakes *every* time! And now, besides Regular and Buckwheat, there's wonderful *new* Aunt Jemima *Buttermilk* Mix to complete the pancake picture in your pantry. So buy all three and get your

plastic, self-measuring, Aunt Jemima shaker *free!* Just send the box-tops from all three mixes, with your name and address, to Shaker, Box 1088, Chicago 77, Ill. Offer expires at midnight, December 31, 1957.

AUNT JEMIMA

Aunt Jemima Pancakes ad, with free shaker offer, *Better Homes and Gardens,* November 1957. **$5-$7**

Aunt Jemima Shakers, two-piece blue plastic with molded "Aunt Jemima Pancakes" on lid, 1950s. **$25-$28**

Two-piece yellow and white plastic with molded "Aunt Jemima Pancakes" and image on lid, 1950s-1960s. **$22-$25**

Planters Peanuts ad, with fascinating premiums offer, 1950s. **$8-$10**

Planters *Presidents of the United States Paint Book,* 1950s. **$18-$25**

Planters Mr. Peanut Premiums
drinking cup	$18-$20
salt and pepper shakers	
	$25-$28
nut chopper	$22-$25
nut dishes	$28-$35 set
bank	$25-$28

Red plastic items showing minimal wear bring the best prices.

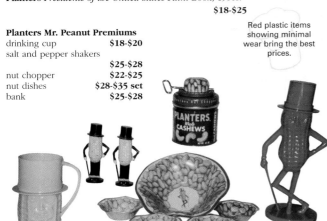

Swift's Allsweet Oleomargarine Box, with sterling silverware offer, 1950s, Swift & Co., Chicago, IL.

$10-$12 each

Playtex Living Gloves Box, with free extra right hand offer, "So flexible you can even pick up a thin dime," 1960s, Intl. Platex Corp., Dover, DE.

$12-$15

Wheaties Box, with Queen Bess silverware offer, 1940s-1950s.

$25-$28

Condition and back cover content are important factors affecting box value. Coupons were included inside every General Mills product.

Silverware Coupons
$5-$8 each
Queen Bess Silverware, three-piece set, 1940s-1950s.
$15-$18

Lipton Promotion Baster Set, with original mailing box, 1950s.

$18-$22

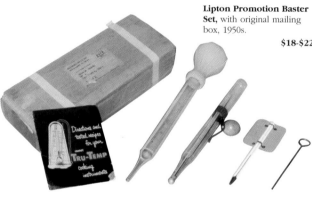

Mazola Promotion Canister Set with Salt and Pepper Shakers, aluminum with copper-toned lids, boxed, 1950s.

$22-$25

Calumet Cookie Cutters, free with purchase of large-sized Calumet Baking Powder, Wear-Ever aluminum, with box, 1940s.

$22-$25

Crisco Shortening, 3-D cookie cutters promotion, plastic cutters by Wecolite, with box and instruction sheet, 1956.

$25-$30

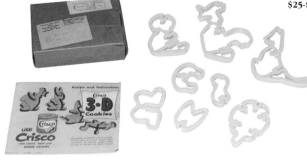

Swift's Allsweet Oleomargarine ad, with sterling silverware
promotion, *Woman's Home Companion,* May 1953.

$2-$5

Lipton Tea ad, with 24-piece picnic set offer, *Woman's Day*, July 1953.

$2-$5

Lipton Promotion 24-piece picnic set.

$18-$25

Lipton Tea Bags Box, 1950s.

$10-$12

Swiftning Shortening ad, with toast glasses offer, *Woman's Day*, June 1952.

$2-$5

Swiftning Shortening Can, 1950s.

$18-$22

Swiftning Shortening Toast Glasses, set of 12, Lucite plastic with original mailing box, 1950s, Swift & Co., Chicago, IL.

$18-$22

Swiftning Shortening ad, with heart-shaped layer cake pans offer, *Woman's Day*, February 1950.

$2-$5

Heart-Shaped Layer Cake Pans, 1950s.

$12-$15

Lipton Tea ad, with cleaverette offer, *Woman's Day*, July 1951.

$2-$5

In 1949, you could get a full-sized cleaver from Duz Detergent for 60 cents.

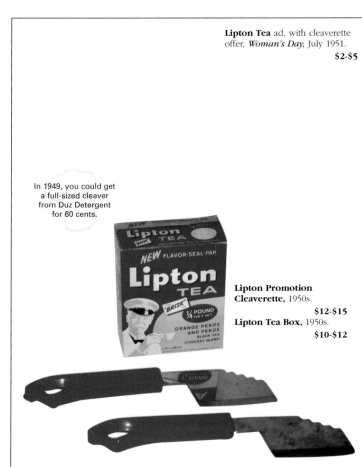

Lipton Promotion Cleaverette, 1950s.

$12-$15

Lipton Tea Box, 1950s.

$10-$12

Mazola Oil ad, with holiday steak knife offer, *Better Homes and Gardens*, July 1956.

$2-$5

Mazola Promotion Holiday Steak Knife Set by Quikut, boxed 1950s.

$20-$25

Sizzling Ideas for better barbecues outdoors or IN

Discover how Mazola® Oil makes everything from salad to sauce—'specially delicious!

Let's have Shish Kebab! Quick marinating sauce: Take a clove of garlic, ½ cup of Mazola Oil, ¼ cup vinegar, ½ teaspoon salt, 1 teaspoon dry mustard, ⅛ teaspoon Worcestershire sauce and a dash of cayenne. Blend. Pour over cubed meat in shallow dish. Let stand 1 to 2 hours.

Skewer chunks of beef or lamb alternately with cubes of vegetables. Brush with marinating sauce. Place on pre-heated grill or broiler. Broil 10 to 15 minutes, until tender.

Approach your barbecue with a spirit of adventure. But remember, for barbecuing... for baking...for salad dressings...nothing gives food wonderful "golden goodness" like Mazola Oil.

EASY-DO BARBECUE SAUCE

2 tbsp. Mazola Oil	½ tsp. salt
¼ cup chopped onions	2 tbsp. lemon juice
1 tbsp. Worcestershire	or vinegar
sauce	½ cup water
1 tbsp. sugar	1 cup chili sauce

Cook Mazola and onions over low heat, stirring frequently, about 10 minutes. Add remaining ingredients and simmer 15 minutes, stirring occasionally. Remove from heat. Makes about 1½ cups.

Barbecued chicken: Brush chicken with Mazola and place on grill or broiler rack. Cook, turning often. Baste frequently with barbecue sauce during cooking. Cook until tender. Serve with hot barbecue sauce.

Hint to remember—Brush your meat or fish with Mazola *before* you place it on the grill. This keeps meat from sticking. Mazola makes all meat delicious and juicy on the inside—crusty and brown on the outside.

COUNTRY GARDEN DRESSING
(Make it right in the bowl!!)

½ clove garlic	¼ tsp. Worcestershire
¼ tsp. prepared	sauce
mustard	1½ tbsp. vinegar
1 tsp. salt	4 tbsp. Mazola
Few grains pepper	Salad Oil

Drop garlic clove in salad bowl. Add prepared mustard, salt and a few pepper grains. Blend thoroughly with fork. Add Worcestershire sauce, vinegar and Mazola. Beat with fork until thoroughly mixed...now add mixed greens and toss. For more than 4 servings, double recipe.

New! Exclusive offer
HOLIDAY STEAK KNIVES
set of **6** for $**1**⁰⁰ and 1 Mazola label

Wonderful new idea...6 Quikut steak knives with 6 assorted pastel-colored handles! Beautiful with any setting. Handles are guaranteed not to come off. Extra sharp stainless steel blades. A marvelous value. Use this handy order form.

MAZOLA, BOX 22B, FREMONT, OHIO

I am enclosing $_____ and _____ Mazola Oil label(s). Please send postpaid _____ set(s) of 6 Holiday steak knives, assorted handles. (Send $1.00 and one label for each set.)

NAME _____
 (Please Print)

STREET _____

CITY _____ STATE _____

Offer expires August 30, 1956. Offer void in any state, territory, or municipality where prohibited, taxed or otherwise restricted.

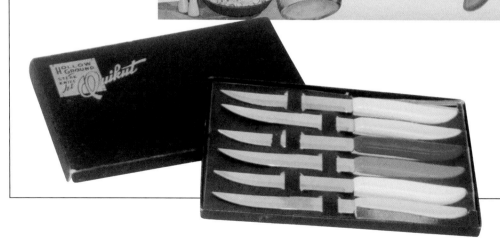

Gold Medal Flour, cookie cutters promotion, free with 25-lb. Purchase, plastic cutters by Hutzler Mfg. Co.

$12-$15

Super Absorbant ScotTowels, "Strong even when wet," in package, 1950s.

$15-$18

ScotTowels Towel Rack, plastic, 1950s.

$15-$18

Accent Third Shaker Set, glass with plastic lid and holder, "Accent makes food flavors sing," boxed, 1950s.

$35-$40

Accent Tin, 1/4 lb. 1950s, International Minerals and Chemical Co., Chicago, IL.

$12-$15

Good Luck Margarine Box, 1950s.

$8-$10

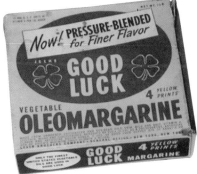

Good Luck Margarine Measuring Guides, plastic, 1950s.

$5-$7 each

There's a special elegance to serving soup!

... with this beautiful ladle offered to you <u>exclusively</u> by *Campbell's*

So beautiful — you'll use it with your handsomest soup tureen, to ladle out a great favorite, like Campbell's Tomato Soup.

Use it with this new serving trick — bringing Campbell's Cream of Mushroom right to the table in pretty cook-and-serve ware.

Use it when you try out a new idea — like serving Campbell's wonderful Cream of Chicken Soup from a chafing dish or buffet server.

Use it to serve ice-cold Campbell's Beef Broth—refreshing and delicious.

Yours for $1.00 RETAIL VALUE $3.50

This silver-plated soup ladle was adapted from a Paul Revere design by Bailey, Banks & Biddle, Philadelphia silversmiths since 1832

PAUL REVERE created the design of the handle. You can see his original today in the famous Boston Museum of Fine Arts. Bailey, Banks & Biddle adapted it — the honored Philadelphia silversmiths whose masterpieces have been treasured through five American generations. Now you can own this beautiful 9½-inch ladle for just $1.00 and a label from your favorite Campbell's Soup. Remember birthdays, showers, weddings, graduations! There's no limit to the number of ladles you can send for. Just send $1.00 and one Campbell's Soup label for each one you order.

SOUP LADLE. P.O. Box 72, Mount Vernon 10, New York

Send _____ silver-plated ladle(s) designed by Bailey, Banks & Biddle. I enclose $1.00 and one Campbell's Soup label for each.

Name _____

Address _____

City _____ State _____

Offer expires September 30, 1957, and may be withdrawn earlier. Offer good only in continental U.S.A., Alaska and Hawaii. Subject to state and local regulations; void if taxed, restricted or forbidden by law. *Please send cash, check, or money order.* Sorry! No stamps! No C.O.D.'s!

Campbell's Soup ad, with silver-plated ladle offer, *Better Homes and Gardens,* April 1957.

$2-$5

Campbell's Soup Can, sealed, 1950s.

$18-$20

Campbell's Promotion Soup Ladle, silver-plated design by Bailey, Banks & Biddle, 1950s.

$22-$25

Chapter 29

Toy Sets

When looking through a toy catalog from the 1940s or 1950s you're likely to see quite a number of toy sets available. Many varieties of dish sets and the lesser-seen toy baking and cooking sets were made. Toy sets appeal to many collectors and have a great deal of charm due to their reduced scale, fun graphics, and scarcity. Their allure is usually reflected in pricing and values. Almost every vintage toy set was played with at some point. Sometimes all you can hope to find are sets that were less played with. I looked for over 18 months before I happened across a nice Revere set at a show. By that point the pricing did not deter me.

Complete Aunt Jemima baking sets from the 1950s are even harder to find. In fact, they may set you back several hundred dollars. When collecting toy sets, the search and variety are part of the fun, as well as discovering unusual examples. In the 1950s they even made a miniature Can-O-Matic set with plastic cans to open!

Merry Manufacturing Co. ad showing four toys

Revere Ware toy cooking utensils ad from *Woman's Day,* December 1955.

$5-$7

Carton can be used as a play stove.

Miniature Revere Ware Utensils, copper clad stainless steel with plastic handles, "Just like mom's," boxed, 1950s, Revere Copper and Brass Inc, Rome Mfg. Div., Rome, NY.

$200-$225

Kay Stanley's Pillsbury Cake Mix Set, with real food, a complete baking set for junior cooks, boxed, 1950s, Model Craft Inc., Chicago, IL.

$75-$100

Gotham Happy Day Outing Kit, plastic table service for four with metal box, "just for girls and boys," 1950s.

$35-$40

Kiddykook Aluminum Toys, "Safe, Durable, Recommended by leading educators," boxed, 1950s, Aluminum Specialty Co., Manitowoc, WI.

$25-$30

Mirro Aluminum Toys, "Like Mothers, safe, unbreakable, rust-proof, Play grown-up as a charming hostess," boxed with recipe book, 1940s.

$75-$100

Tag states this set was made of alternate materials due to the war effort.

Small Fry Pastry Set, plastic with wood rolling pin and metal beater, boxed, 1950s, Pressman Toy Corp., New York, NY.

$100-$125

Dolly's Kitchen Closet, "Like mom's," with contents, 1950s, Merry Manufacturing Co., Cincinnati, OH.

$25-$30

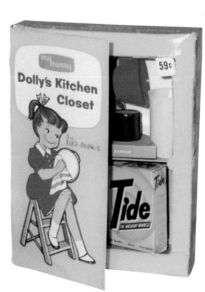

Chapter 30

A Plastic Wonderland

Nearly one hundred years of advances preceded the 1950s plastics revolution in housewares and consumer goods. The first discoveries were motivated by the need to replace limited natural materials such as ivory and tortoiseshell. In the 1860s, a $10,000 challenge to find a substitute for ivory billiard balls led John Hyatt on a path of experimentation resulting in the discovery of celluloid. Though not well suited for billiards, it found ready acceptance when used for buttons, combs, umbrella handles, and other "fancy goods." Advances in processing led to celluloid's expanded role in photographic film by the turn of the century. By the 1940s, Catalin had surpassed Bakelite for many uses, but America's involvement in World War II began to radically alter the availability and development of plastics. Nylon fabric, which was ideally suited for parachutes, cords, and other high strength applications was banned for civilian uses resulting in a huge shortage of women's hosiery that continued for months after the war was over. In early 1946 when new supplies of nylon hosiery finally started showing up in stores, Gimbel's allotment of 25,000 pairs attracted an equivalent number of mostly women customers, all bound for the 5th floor hosiery department.

A more durable hard plastic was discovered by Leo Baekeland in 1907, and was quickly named Bakelite after its esteemed creator. Bakelite first found acceptance for use in electrical insulators, but other applications followed. By the 1930s, it was the preferred material for a wide range of household items. Cameras, telephones, adding machines, and other items that could benefit from a streamlined design were molded out of Bakelite. Later in the 1930s another compound, Catalin, similar to Bakelite but offering the advantage of wider color selection, found acceptance as a material for utensil handles, radios, and other consumer goods.

Further discoveries and process improvements during the war years, arising in part from the urgent need to find a synthetic rubber, led to the first mass production of styrene and discovery of polyethylene. These plastics offered several advantages over Catalin and earlier compounds, such as ease of processing and cost. By war's end, Dow, Monsanto, and other companies with excess production capacity of styrene, tried to increase demand by creating special "programs" to advance its use in just about every imaginable household object.

By the 1950s, a typical consumer, ready to outfit a new suburban house, was eager to embrace plastic items as they were introduced. Having obvious beauty, utility, and cost savings, buyers could temporarily overlook some minor drawbacks. Styrene had the tendency to crack or break, particularly when dropped, while polyethylene's surface would sometimes feel sticky to the touch and attract dirt. But this was just a little drizzle at the start of a booming plastics parade. Plastics were hip and modern, and objects like the 1953 Corvette with its reinforced fiberglass body held every adolescent youth in a suspended trance at the GM Motorama. Toys, games, and novelties of all sorts also benefited by a plasticized magic wand. For a time in the 1950s, production of Wham-O's Hula Hoop devoured a large percentage of the newly available compound high density polyethylene. When the clamor finally subsided, a follow up offering, the "Pluto Platter" Frisbee, did even better with sales never letting up.

The future could indeed be a plastic one as demonstrated in 1957 with Monsanto's plastic House of the Future at Disneyland, or at least until its novelty wore off in the late 1960s. But plastics did offer American consumers an abundant pie, preferably served up in a durable, lightweight, low cost, plastic pie holder, available just about everywhere.

Plaskon Closures ARE STOPPERS IN MORE WAYS THAN ONE!

THERE are three major features which distinguish Plaskon Molded Color for closures: utility, economy, and attractiveness.

Plaskon molding materials are plastics that are especially resistant to the chemical and physical action of a wide variety of products that must be packaged. Plaskon is completely impervious to the effects of alcohol, acetone, or other common organic solvents. It is not affected by oils, fats or greases. Because it is odorless, tasteless and inert, it has no effect upon any products with which it comes into contact.

Plaskon can be molded in large quantities at very economical prices. Distinctive designs and shapes can be secured to give new individuality to packages.

Plaskon is available in a wide range of beautiful, permanent colors that improve the appearance of any container, catch the eye and help make sales. We can give you helpful assistance in suggesting designs, qualified Plaskon molders, and technical advice so that you can efficiently adapt Plaskon Molded Color to your manufacturing and sales programs.

PLASKON DIVISION, Libbey-Owens-Ford Glass Company, 2125 Sylvan Ave., Toledo 6, Ohio
In Canada: Canadian Industries, Ltd., Montreal

Plaskon Bottle Closures ad, Libbey-Owens-Ford Glass Co., 1940s. **$2-$5**

"We've Been Using *Catalin* for Twenty Years...It's Our Best Handle Material"

This long term expression of Catalin-confidence comes from principals of The Washburn Co., Worcester, Mass. For two decades, this company's famous lines of "Androck" ware have been almost exclusively Catalin-handled . . . and at the point-of-sale still are consistently Catalin-identified. Other leading houseware–manufacturers too, are as enthusiastically outspoken. Catalin Cast Phenolics are definitely their first choice for handles and knobs . . . and for these important reasons . . .

• Catalin will not burn . . . it is absolutely safe.

• Catalin is sanitary . . . it will not absorb or be affected by household acids, cleansers, grease, etc.

• Catalin is tough . . . it can take rough treatment, won't soften, and will not scratch or chip readily.

• Catalin, *the Gem of Plastics* . . . is all color, clear through. Its finish is permanent.

ANNOUNCING A NEW *Heat-Resistant*
Catalin CAST PHENOLIC
BOILING-WATER PROOF...CAN BE STERILIZED

This new material opens a new world of COLOR for Cooking Utensils and Electrical Appliances. Possesses exceptional strength, heat and chemical resistance properties. Complete information and samples available. Write today to Dept. HW.

In the interest of increased sales and supreme consumer satisfaction, retailers should insist on genuine Catalin-handled ware . . . Its twenty year service-reputation, is in itself a warranty! Manufacturers concerned with handle problems are invited to send for our free 16 page catalog. Write today to Dept. HW

CATALIN
THE GEM OF PLASTICS
Catalin

CATALIN CORPORATION OF AMERICA • ONE PARK AVENUE, NEW YORK 16, N. Y.

Catalin Plastic ad featuring an assortment of Androck kitchen utensils, "It's our best handle material," *House Furnishing Review,* July 10, 1948. The advantages of Catalin over Bakelite were obvious, however, consumer awareness of the Bakelite name was hard to overcome. **$2-$5**

STYRON

(DOW POLYSTYRENE)

IF YOUR eye were looking through the crystal-clear cube, you would see the fascinating future of a remarkable plastic development. This cube is STYRON*—Dow's tradename for polystyrene which it pioneered and produces.

STYRON is a highly efficient electrical insulator and is resistant to alcohol, acids and alkalies. Precision moldings from this material have high dimensional stability. STYRON is but one of several Dow plastics —all possessing endless possibilities for new and useful applications when peace returns.

Behind STYRON is the water-white liquid—styrene —an essential ingredient of synthetic rubber and one of Dow's great contributions to Victory.

CHEMICALS INDISPENSABLE TO INDUSTRY AND VICTORY

THE DOW CHEMICAL COMPANY, MIDLAND, MICHIGAN

New York • St. Louis • Chicago • San Francisco • Los Angeles • Seattle • Houston

*Trade Mark Reg. U. S. Pat. Off.

Styron was Dow's brand name for styrene plastic, also known as polystyrene.

Styron Plastic ad from Dow Chemical Co., 1940s.

$2-$5

Liberty Magazine, December 22, 1945, with cover illustration by Del Holcomb. The eager associate behind the counter is trying to "sell" a discriminating lady customer some nylon stockings. This scene must have seemed laughingly unreal in its day, considering the shortage of nylon hosiery prevalent at the time.

$6-$8

What I told a young hostess
about _informal_ entertaining

Look for this label on the better
housewares you buy

—another in the big MONSANTO family of plastics

SERVING INDUSTRY . . . WHICH SERVES MANKIND

Monsanto Chemical Company, Plastics Division,
Room 305, Springfield 2, Mass. Lustrex: Reg. U.S.Pat.Off.

Monsanto's Lustrex Styrene Plastic ad with "Modern Living Consultant," Marion
Palmer, featuring styrene plastic serving pieces. *Good Housekeeping*, April 1952.

$2-$5

Durable 8-oz. tumblers for kitchen or bathroom use . . . 10c

3-pint Hande batter bowls; large handle and pouring lip . . . 69c

Salt 'n pepper range set. 4-in. shakers hold plenty! 59c

Whisk this 2-qt. covered jug from table to refrigerator! 98c

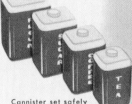

Cannister set safely stores flour, sugar, coffee, tea. Set . . . $3.49

Sturdy 4-compartment cutlery tray keeps silverware tidy . . . 79c

the Best Buy

FOR MY KITCHEN

INEXPENSIVE
COLORFUL
PLASTICS
HOUSEWARES

Guaranteed by Good Housekeeping

No doubt about it . . . the best buys in housewares are plastics! And the best buys in plastics are made of STYRON, the famous Dow polystyrene! STYRON housewares are practical, durable, colorful . . . and so inexpensive, too!

Where to buy them:

GO TO ANY OF THESE
LEADING VARIETY STORES
FOUND COAST TO COAST

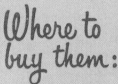

. . . more than 1700 locally-owned Ben Franklin Stores

. . . the newly added Butler Brothers Stores: big, modern!

Butler Brothers own Scott Stores everywhere

. . . thousands of other independent variety stores

BUTLER BROTHERS
CHICAGO, ILLINOIS

Refrigerator jars for left-overs; space-savers! 3 in set . . . 69c

Versatile cake tray with twist-on lock lift cover $2.19

Oriental temple with hanging planter; plant not included 98c

Hostess set with covered sugar, creamer, 2 sets of shakers . . 98c

Measuring cup set; 4 sizes from ¼ cup to 1 cup, nested 29c

Plants look prettier in these colorful pots with saucers 49c

Dow Styron plastic ad featuring Colorful Plastics Housewares. *Good Housekeeping*, November 1951.

$5-$7

for your kitchen and refrigerator

new PLASTICS ideas to lighten your chores and brighten your Home!

Yes, plastic housewares . . . made of STYRON . . . give modern housewives plenty of time for leisure. Handy, convenient for storing or serving—from refrigerator to table without using unnecessary dishes. Note too how the new "soft tone" colors add a fresh decor to your kitchen or table setting.

MADE OF STYRON® A DOW PLASTIC

Handy 2½-qt. Pitcher; asstd. colors . . . . 98¢

High dome Cake Cover on 11½" Tray 1.98

Quart size Shaker for drinks or juices . . . . 59¢

Smart Bread Box, keeps bread fresher 1.29

3-pc. Refrig. Set . . . 98¢ Individual jars: 25¢, 49¢

4-pc. Canister Set, modern design . . . . Set, 2.98

4-pc. Tumbler Set in asstd. colors . . . Set, 39¢

Knife and Fork Tray; 3 sizes . . . . 59¢, 79¢, 98¢

Attractive 5-pc. Salad 'n Snack Set 1.49

Flavor Server Set for relish, sauces, etc . . . 98¢

Salt 'n Pepper Set, range size . . . . . Set 49¢

Attractive Creamer 'n Sugar Tray Set . . . . 98¢

for home decoration

Modern design watering can, 14-oz. size . . . . 49¢

Spinning Wheel Planter 98¢
African Violet Flower Pot *49¢
Flower Pot with Saucer*, in 4 sizes . . 25¢, 35¢, 49¢ & 59¢
(*As illustrated in use)

for your table

Buy all your plastic needs at your nearby . . . **BEN FRANKLIN SCOTT** *or* **BUTLER BROTHERS** *store*

BEN FRANKLIN   SCOTT   BUTLER BROTHERS

BUTLER BROTHERS
Headquarters in Chicago

Dow Styron Plastics ad from *Better Homes and Gardens,* 1950s. **$2-$5**

PLASTICS -AMERICAN AS APPLE PIE

We're all living with plastics today! Nation-wide enthusiasm has elevated versatile, colorful and economical plastics to key materials that brighten modern living. Yes, in national acceptance, plastics are as American as apple pie!

Since Dow's entrance into the world of plastics, it has, through continuing research and development, come to be a major producer in the industry. Dow plastics are adding new color, beauty and serviceability to countless products we use every day.

STYRON (Dow Polystyrene) is transforming numerous practical housewares into exciting new beauties, leads the

parade in toyland, and serves well in essential parts for radios, refrigerators and fine cars. ETHOCEL (Dow Ethylcellulose), another Dow plastic with special qualities, provides beauty and extreme serviceability in its host of industrial applications. SARAN, still a third member of the Dow plastic family, is extruded and woven into modern fabrics. It sets a new pace for beauty and durability in

auto seat covers, upholstery, luggage and screening.

Across the land, Americans welcome the friendly touch plastics give to daily living. And Dow's aim is to bring you the full benefit of its progress in plastics and other useful products of chemistry.

THE DOW CHEMICAL COMPANY
MIDLAND, MICHIGAN

Look for the STYRON Label

It's the buy-word for better plastics housewares and toys in chain, department and variety stores across the country. And look for saran in smartly styled, durable seat covers at your dealer's.

DOW
CHEMICALS
INDISPENSABLE TO INDUSTRY AND AGRICULTURE

Dow Styron plastic ad "American as apple pie." *Saturday Evening Post*, March 11, 1950.

$2-$5

Telephone with Bakelite handset and metal body from Western Electric, 1930s-1940s.

$65-$75

Older telephones are attracting a growing number collectors, this example was "rescued" from a trash bin in the early 1990s.

Kodak Bullet Camera with a molded Bakelite plastic case, boxed, 1930s.

$40-$45

An early example of product streamlining, this camera showed how plastic materials could add beauty and utility.

This early set of corncob holders is prized by collectors for its angular Art Deco lines and bright plastic colors, also available in yellow or green.

Kob Knobs, set of eight, Bakelite (Catalin) plastic, 1930s-1940s, C.J. Schneider Mfg. Co., Toledo, OH.

$55-$65

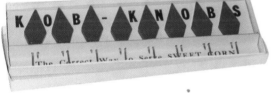

Cookie Cutters, bridge set of four, Bakelite "Plastic moulded," boxed, 1930s-1940s.

$18-$22

Plasticville Ranch House Model, "The original plastic village," boxed, 1950s, Bachmann Bros. Inc.

$28-$35

Wham-O Frisbee, polyethylene, "Flies like a plane, spins like a gyroscope, America's favorite game of catch," in package, 1967.

$18-$22

Plasticville 5 and 10 Store Model, 1950s, Bachmann Bros. Inc., Philadelphia, PA.

$25-$35

The Plasticville model series was made for use with scale model railroad layouts.

Chapter 31

Lustro-Ware/Columbus Plastic Products

In Columbus, Ohio, a struggling plastics molding firm was taken over by an eager Harvard graduate, Gebhard W. Keny. This change was the nucleus for the start of Columbus Plastic Products. Early product designations, such as the Zippo line, fell by the wayside in favor of the Lustro-Ware name. The introduction of a molded styrene plastic cutlery tray in the 1940s revolutionized its entire product category. The future of Columbus Plastics Products seemed bright. After the creation of an in-house design department, other innovative products were introduced. One of the first was a plastic canister set having a simple straightforward design, block lettering, and rounded, easy-to-clean inside corners. This set was followed by a line of matching pieces including bread boxes, shakers, and dispensers that helped set a uniform modern style for American households. The basic colors of red and yellow were augmented by other hues, so that the products from Columbus Plastics fit right in with the ongoing color schemes of the day.

Columbus Plastic Products and Lustro-Ware continued to be a leader in the 1950s and diversified into polyethylene items and larger molded pieces such as laundry baskets, trash containers, and other household necessities. Their main facility on Mound street in Columbus, Ohio, more than tripled in size within a span of a few years. By the late 1950s, most of the products were being made in the softer shades of pink, turquoise, and light yellow. Continued success with plastics molding innovation resulted in the development of intricate molds capable of making lacey napkin holders and plastic doilies available at five and dime stores for 19 cents. In its heyday, the Lustro-Ware line boasted the availability of, "Over 100 stylized items to brighten the home."

The classic design period at Columbus Plastic Products ended around 1959, when the more abstract lettering and designs of the Elegante line were introduced. In a sense, the simplicity of the product shape seemed to be upstaged by the ornate graphics, and the overall effect didn't seem to work as well. However, the Lustro-Ware line continued to be successful and still featured older as well as new products. In 1966, Columbus Plastic Products was acquired by the Borden company. After additional product changes, including the adoption of avocado green and harvest gold to its color palette, Lustro-Ware's design direction while under Borden became diluted and wasn't able to recapture its former success.

Today, collectors seem drawn to the Lustro-Ware name, distinctly molded on the bottom of most of the products. The usual collecting pattern is for someone to acquire a canister set or other item and when a matching accessory piece is found, a collection is born. The most popular period for Lustro-Ware items spans roughly 1950 to 1960 and nearly any item from that time period in nice condition has collector interest. Most appealing are canister sets and other ensemble pieces with the classic block lettering bright and intact, and without cracks or other flaws. Expect to pay a premium price for boxed, mint-condition items and harder-to-find accessories like towel dispensers. Its not unusual for a Lustro-Ware "spice" rack, that is often used to display 1950s Aunt Jemima spice containers, to sell for upwards of $100 on the Internet and for period catalogs to do much better. But these items are the exception, and with the number of objects in circulation, Lustro-Ware is truly a collectible available for anyone showing an interest.

Zippo Utility Line, plastic encased "For kitchen, bathroom, basement, etc.," boxed, 1940s, Columbus Plastic Products Co.

$22-$25

Lustro-Ware Clothesline, stock #R1, "Convenient, practical, for drying hosiery, lingerie, etc.," boxed, 1950s.

$22-$25

Lustro-Ware Utensil Trays, styrene plastic, available in a range of colors, 1950s.

$15-$20 each

Lustro-Ware Spice Cabinet, "Holds eight to ten cans of spices," with insert card, 1950s.

$35-$40

Lustro-Ware Relish and Bread Tray, styrene plastic, with label, 1950s.

$18-$22

Unmarked plastic usually escapes the notice of collectors; dark green is unusual for Lustro-Ware.

Lustro-Ware Egg Trays, compact, 12 egg capacity, 1950s.

$18-$22

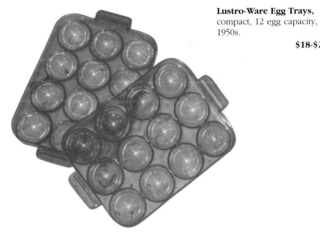

Lustro-Ware Egg Trays, Oblong, 12 egg capacity, #L-$31, 1950s.

$15-$20

Lustro-Ware Double-size Coasters, set of four, for bottle and glass, with label, 1950s.

$18-$22

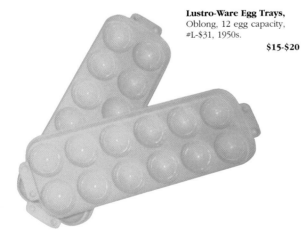

These coasters were butter & cheese dish bottoms put to an additional use, the product name on the bottom was XXX'd out at the factory.

Lustro-Ware, America's Foremost Line, front cover from 1951
Lustro-Ware Catalog, collection of Internet seller Marsha
Brandom. Catalog with letter, price list, and envelope.

$125-$150

Lustro-Ware Watering Can, styrene plastic with clear bottoms, #P-10, 1950s.

$25-$30

Unusual shape is hard to find in nice condition.

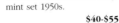

Lustro-Ware Ice Bucket, double wall styrene plastic with lid, #112, 1950s, in brown & cream $18-$22; red & white.

$22-$28

Lustro-Ware Canister Set, mint set 1950s.

$40-$55

Sets free from flaws with bright lettering bring the best prices. Unused, boxed sets usually sell at a premium.

Lustro-Ware Bread Box, #B20L, 1950s.

$35-$45

Lustro-Ware Recipe Box, styrene plastic, #B-25, 1950s.

$22-$25

Mint condition and original, unused cards add to value.

Lustro-Ware Salt & Pepper Shakers, small table size, "Easy to fill twist-lock covers," #SS-2, mint set.

$12-$15

Add $8-$10 for unused, in package examples.

Lustro-Ware Dispenser, for wax paper, paper towels, and foils, stock #H-15, "Handy to use, Always beautiful," boxed, unused, 1950s.

$65-$75

Popular matching piece with collectors, wear to lettering is common, red usually sells for a premium.

L-35 BUTTER DISH

¼ pound size with snug fitting crystal cover for refrigerator storage. Tray will not tip when butter is sliced. Colors match other refrigerator dishes. Size 2¾"x6¼"x2¾".

L-36 REFRIGERATOR DISH

Housewives like its light weight, compactness, and elimination of breakage hazards. Snug fitting crystal cover and crystal or sparkling colorful bottoms. Easily cleaned and safe in hottest faucet water. Dishes may be stacked as shown on the right 4"x4"x3" size.

L-37 REFRIGERATOR DISH

Large 4"x8"x3" size matches other refrigerator dishes. Recess on cover keeps stacked dishes secure. Also ideal for candy or gift boxes. Crystal and sparkling kitchen colors.

L-40 CRISPER

Adds extra capacity to refrigerator. Handy for home, restaurant or picnic use. Snug fitting crystal view cover and crystal or opaque colored bottom. Size 13"x8⅛"x4-9/16".

L-45 REFRIGERATOR PITCHER

Handsome for table use, compact for storage. Generous 2 quart capacity plus ice. Large opening permits easy cleaning. Swing action lid covers opening and spout with ice retainer strip. Light, yet practically non-breakable. Size 6½"x4⅛"x 6¾". Popular kitchen colors.

RS-1 REFRIGERATOR SET

Comprising of two L-36 and one L-37. Dishes stack as illustrated. All crystal or crystal covers and opaque colored bottoms. Cellophane wrapped.

RS-1B Refrigerator set (4 pieces) comprising of two L-36, one L-37, and one L-35 butter dish. Cellophane wrapped.

RS-2 Refrigerator set (6 pieces) consisting of four L-36, and two L-37. Set individually boxed.

RS-2B Refrigerator set (7 pieces) consisting of four L-36, two L-37 and one L-35 butter dish. Boxed.

L-50 SPICE CABINET

Holds 8 to 10 spice cans on any wall, door, shelf or table top. Also appropriate for toiletries in the bathroom or as a what-not shelf. Solid back protects wall surfaces and ledge keeps containers from jarring off. Size 5¾"x6⅝"x3". Furnished with visual merchandising insert. Assorted colors.

L-51 SPICE RACK

Keeps spice tins orderly and handy. Holds five regular size containers. Mounts on any surface, slot holes for easy removal. Popular kitchen colors. Size 13⅝"x1¾"x2¼".

L-55 CLOTHES SPRINKLER

Lightweight, non-tipping, practically non-breakable, easy to hold. Positive snap-on, snap-off cap for quick filling. Crystal body, opaque colored bottom and cap. Size 6⅛"x3¼".

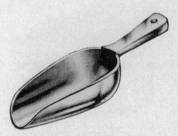

L-60 SCOOP

All purpose design with high sides for maximum volume and tapered spout for easy pouring without spilling. Ideal for foods, bulky materials, including chemicals. Will not rust or corrode. Length 6½". Popular kitchen colors.

L-70 BREAD BASKET

Round design of attractive open pattern with solid bottom to catch crumbs. For serving rolls, bread or fruit in the home . . . restaurant, too! Sanitary, easy to clean, safe in hottest faucet water. 9" in diameter, 2½" deep. Popular colors.

The Line that bears the GOOD HOUSEKEEPING GUARANTY SEAL

- 5 -

An assortment of items shown in a 1950s *Lustro-Ware Catalog*. Customers sending for a free catalog also received a price list and available mail-order outlets.

Lustro-Ware Loop Towel Holder, styrene plastic, #L-27. Saves space, decorative, for kitchen or bathroom, on card, 1950s.

$18-$22

Red units are premium priced.

Lustro-Ware Paper Towel Holder, styrene plastic, spring action brackets, #H-10, durable, economical, convenient, on card, 1950s.

$15-$18

Lustro-Ware Paper Towel Holder, later version 1950s-1960s.

$10-$12

Lustro-Ware Refrigerator Set, three-piece, safe, guaranteed unbreakable for 1 year, in package, yellow, 1950s.

$25-$30

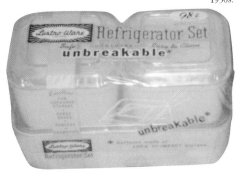

Lustro-Ware Refrigerator Set, three-piece, safe, guaranteed unbreakable for 1 year, in package, Red with styron labels.

$25-$28

Lustro-Ware Pie Box, clear styrene marked made in USA, #B-40, "keeps pie tasty fresh," with label, 1950s-1960s.

$18-$20

Lustro-Ware Salad Tongs, styrene plastic, #T-40, "Exclusive one piece spring action design," with label, 1950s.

$18-$25

I found these tongs on the Internet. Although most items for sale on line are listed under Lustro-Ware, with the hyphen, additional entries can usually be found under Lustroware.

Lustro-Ware Screw Top Decanter, polyethylene, jumbo 70 oz., 1950s-1960s.

$15-$18

The screw-top lid is awkward to use.

Front cover from mid-1950s Lustro-Ware catalog.
Catalog with letter, price list, and envelope.

$125-$150

Lustro-Ware Refrigerator Pitcher, two-piece styrene plastic body with swing action lid, 2 quart capacity, #L-45, 1950s.

green, unused with early sticker **$25-$30**

yellow, with sticker **$22-$28**

red, with sticker **$25-$30**

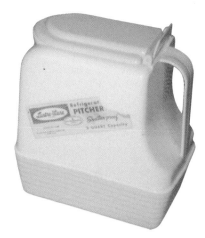

Lustro-Ware Table Pitcher, styrene plastic, #L-46, solid yellow 1950s.

$18-$22

Lustro-Ware Table Pitcher, styrene plastic, Blue and white with transfer decoration 1950s-1960s.

$15-$20

Front cover of Lustro-Ware Lacecraft booklet, 1958.

$15-$18

Plastic Doilies, in package.
6" white **$6-$10**
4" pink **$8-$10**

Lustro-Ware Doily Clasps, 48 polyethylene, for lacecraft creations, on blister card, 1950s-1960s.

$8-$10

Lustro-Ware Juicer, one-piece polyethylene, #L-13, 1950s.

$10-$15

Available in several colors.

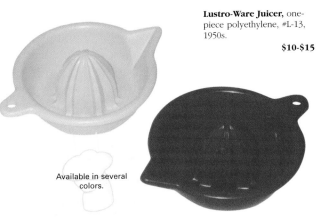

For MORE SALES and PROFITS it's *Lustro-Ware*

the complete GUARANTEED* Line of matching
"FLEXIBLE" and "RIGID" Plastic Housewares

NRHA APPROVED DISPLAY of Lustro-Ware taken in NRHA Merchandising Laboratory

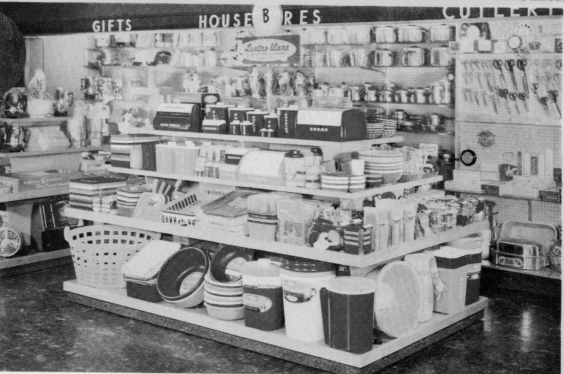

ONE SOURCE for Complete Matching Line.
A colorful Lustro-Ware housewares center is a real traffic builder . . . here's where folks regularly shop for popular priced "FLEXIBLE" and "RIGID" plastic household necessities. Homemakers prefer the smart matching style and top quality found in Lustro-Ware. They buy with complete confidence because they see its guaranteed* UNBREAKABLE service advertised in their favorite magazines.

Concentrate on *Lustro-Ware* for TOP VOLUME with the highest profit margin in housewares.
Feature the ONE and ONLY COMPLETE LINE of over 175 matching household staples in both "FLEXIBLE" and "RIGID" plastic. Lustro-Ware advertising and full color labeling create impulse purchases—invite more sales for other items.

Eliminate off-brand lines and costly mark-downs—make Lustro-Ware your one-order source for simplified stock control. SAVE ON FREIGHT . . . more effective merchandising, too!

SELL EVEN MORE with FREE Shopper Stopping Display Materials. Identify your store as the Lustro-Ware shopping center of your trading area. Free banners, posters and statement enclosures along with newspaper ads and TV spots to tie-in with seasonal Lustro-Ware national advertising. For sales and profits always feature Lustro-Ware.

COLUMBUS PLASTIC PRODUCTS, INC., COLUMBUS, OHIO

*Product replacement or refund of money if consumer is not satisfied with any Lustro-Ware product.

National Consumer ADVERTISING
Sells *Lustro-Ware* to homemakers everywhere

Seldom seen color advertising piece from Lustro-Ware. A similar assortment of Lustro-Ware items found today would be a financial windfall.

Ad page showing National Hardware Association approved Lustro-Ware store display from Hardware Age, mid-1950s.

$20-$22

Lustro-Ware Napkin Holders, 1950s, yellow, lattice vine design, styrene plastic, #H-5.

$12-$15

Lustro-Ware Napkin Holders, 1950s, Red, basketweave design, #H-9.

$18-$20

Lustro-Ware Napkin Holders, 1950s, yellow, flower basket design, #H-7.

$12-$15

Unmarked colander is usually not recognized as Lustro-Ware.

Lustro-Ware Colander, boil-proof rigid polyethylene, "Will not mar sink," with label, 1950s.

$20-$25

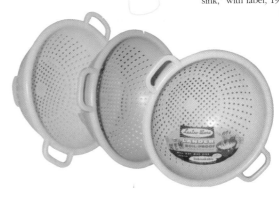

Lustro-Ware Mail Box, styrene plastic with crystal view cover, #B-50, boxed, 1950s-1960s.

$28-$35

Lustro-Ware Ice Bucket, boil-proof polyethylene, insulated, with lid and metallic trim, 1960s.

$18-$22

Lustro-Ware Drain Tray, flexible polyethylene, #L-124S, "Cushion soft and Never gets gummy," with label, 1950s.

$22-$25

Lustro-Ware, full-color ad showing products
available in 1959, *Hardware Age.*

$15-$18

Lustroware Watering Can, rigid polyethylene with embossed design, 1960s-1970s.

$8-$10

Avocado green color helps date this watering can.

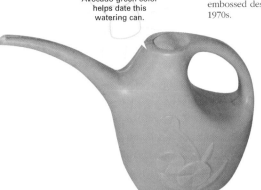

Lustro-Ware Dustpan, styrene plastic, #P-30, "One piece seamless design," 1950s.

$12-$15

Lustro-Ware Watering Can, styrene plastic, 1960s.

$12-$15

Copper color marks this watering can as a later example.

Lustro-Ware Sugar & Creamer Set, boil-proof polyethylene, #CS-16, "Beauty styled, Service tested," boxed, 1950s-1960s.

$18-$22

Lustro-Ware/Borden Measure Cups, set of five polyethylene, in blister package, 1960s-1970s.

$8-$12

Bold 1970s color made earlier plastic kitchenware seem dated.

Lustro-Ware Tissue Dispenser, styrene cover with polyethylene base, gold decorated, 1960s.

$10-$12

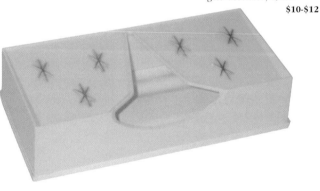

Lustro-Ware Bowl Set, rigid polyethylene, B10, B12, B14, 1960s-1970s.

$12-$15 set

FROM *Elegante* PANTRYWARE to TRASH-TAINERS and 200 other staples

Lustro-Ware **MAKES MORE SALES!**

Start with the fast selling Lustro-Ware pantryware and matching polyethylene housewares—add wonderful Lustro-Ware Trash-Tainers, decorated Waste Baskets, Sprinkling Can, and other exciting new items—mix well with sales-proven Lustro-Ware staples and serve your customers a complete plastic housewares line.

GUARANTEED Customer Satisfaction

You profit again from Lustro-Ware's straight-forward guarantee that applies to all Lustro-Ware items. Value conscious homemakers buy, buy and **BUY WITH ASSURANCE** of replacement or refund if not completely satisfied.

COLUMBUS PLASTIC PRODUCTS, INC., Columbus, Ohio
Sales Offices in principal cities of U.S.A. and Canada

C-124 CS 24-gallon REFUSE-TAINER
Colorful, rust-proof polyethylene. Metal handles flip up to lock cover.
C-112 CS 12-gallon REFUSE-TAINER with locking cover.
C-108 S Rectangular REFUSE-TAINER Saves space. Wonderful for diapers or as picnic beverage cooler. 8-gal. cap.

All sizes also available without covers.

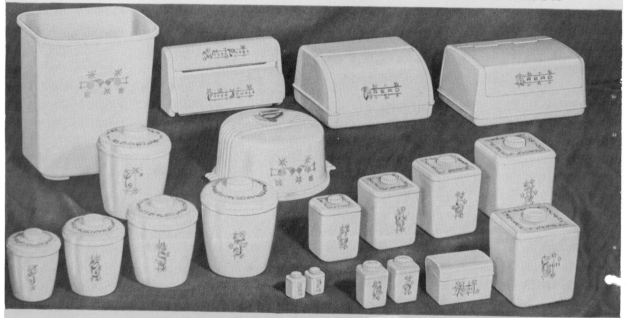

ELEGANTE Metallic Leaf Decorated

Unbreakable, Hi-Impact "Elegante" Pantryware with tarnish-proof gold and chrome embossed metallic leaf decorations. Another *Lustro-Ware* "first" — became an immediate sales sensation for stores everywhere. Feature "Elegante" ensembles and bring 'em back for matching items.

SALES AIDS

FREE newspaper ad mat service, banners, streamers, posters and other display materials that promote your store as "the" place to shop for *Lustro-Ware*. See your supplier today.

Popular Selling Line of
Plastic Lace Doilies, Etc.

Lustro-Ware plastic doilies, place mats and scarfs have the look of fine lace, yet eliminate laundering problems.

4, 6, 8, 10, and 12 inch doilies and 10½ x 15 inch and 12 x 18 inch place mats, packed in sets of 4 of one size and color in printed poly bags. 12 x 36 inch scarf is roll packed singly.

FREE Merchandising Racks sell all sizes and colors

Nationally Advertised and Guaranteed by the **WORLD'S LARGEST** manufacturer of Plastic Housewares

Lustro-Ware full-color ad from 1959 shows the Elegante Metallic Leaf design, *Hardware Age.*

$15-$18

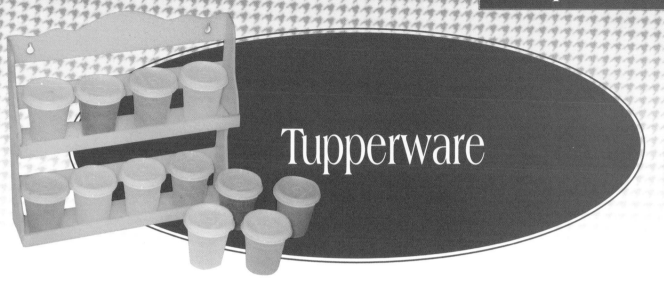

Chapter 32

Tupperware

In 1938, Earl S. Tupper began custom molding plastic items in Farnumsville, MA. By 1945, he produced his first polyethylene product, a seven-ounce juice tumbler. At the time polyethylene was a recently developed plastic compound, with never-before-seen features. It was flexible, durable, opalescent, and suitable for many types of applications.

For consumers, polyethylene was truly a novelty and as its qualities became known, its acceptance grew. This early phase culminated in a full-color feature about Tupperware in the October 1947 issue of *House Beautiful* titled "Fine Art for 39 cents." This boost in awareness helped Earl Tupper expand retail sales, as well as sales in his newly created home party plan division. Earl Tupper soon was promoting his products as being made of "Poly-T," not just ordinary polyethylene, and he also introduced pastel shades. By 1951, Tupperware Home Parties was formed to sell via dealers on the party plan, while retail sales were phased out. It turned out that some features of the product, including the exclusive Tupperware seal, could best be shown and sold through a person-to-person demonstration.

Through the 1950s, Tupperware continued its upward sales trend and additional items and manufacturing capacity were added. In 1956, the simplified elegance of Tupperware was given further acclaim when several containers were put on display in an exhibition at New York's Metropolitan Museum of Art. By 1958, the multimillion dollar Tupperware operation was acquired by Rexall Drug & Chemical Co., later renamed Dart Industries.

Today, Tupperware is somewhat of a sleeper as a collectible. One drawback is difficulty in judging age and scarcity, as well as a seemingly endless supply of the product. Little vintage packaging or point-of-sale materials exist that would interest collectors, since many items were originally sold in a simple plastic bag or tied with a ribbon. Sets in pastel shades and early unusual items are attracting interest on the Internet, however, prices for the most part remain reasonable. It takes an appreciation of object simplicity somewhat akin to admiring Shaker furniture to appreciate Tupperware. However, with the retro allure of pastel shades and its simple functionality, new collectors continue to be attracted to Tupperware.

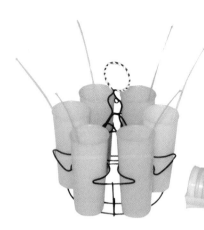

Tupperware Tumblers,
six, 16 oz., in pastel shades
with set of matching
Tumbler Mates stirs, 1950s-
1960s.

$22-$28

Wire Caddy, not
Tupperware, 1950s.

$15-$18

**Tupperware Wagon
Wheel Coaster Set,** six in
pastel shades with handy
Caddy, 1950s-1960s.

$12-$15

Tupperware Pitcher, 2 qt
capacity, 1950s-1960s.
Add $3-$5 if lid is present.

$8-$10

Tupperware Tumblers,
six, 9 oz., in pastel shades,
1950s-1960s.

$18-$20

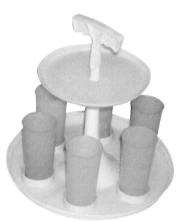

**Tupperware Carousel
Caddy,** holds six tumblers
and has tray for cookies or
other food, 1960s.

$18-$22 without
tumblers

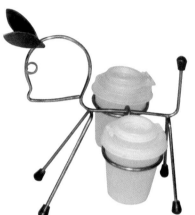

**Tupperware Salt &
Pepper Shakers,** 1950s-
1960s.

$8-$10 set

Wire Deer Caddy, 1950s,
not Tupperware.

$10-$12

Tupperware Salad Tongs,
"Service-talented," boxed,
1950s-1960s.

$15-$18

Tupperware Lazy Susan,
1950s, unmarked styrene
plastic.

$15-$18

Wonderlier Bowl Set, five
sizes in pastel shades with
lids, 1950s-1960s.

$45-$50

Sellers sometimes
combined a three-
piece, small bowl set
with a large bowl set
to form a five-piece
gift set, and kept the
extra bowl for
themselves.
Tupperware sets in
pastel shades appeal
to collectors.

Tupperware Canister Set,
with decoration, 1970s

$18-$22

Other colors available
were lime green,
yellow, and orange.

Small Wonderliers . . . for many types of food preparation, storage and serving . . . 2, 3 and 4-cup capacities. Sets of 3 with seals, $2.59. Bowls are leakproof and stack compactly in tight places. Keeps foods fresh and flavorful longer.

Tupperware . . . the perfect picnic partner!
Tupperware loves picnics . . . and picnickers love Tupperware! It's unbreakable, insect-tight and feather-light. Its high insulating qualities keep salads fresh and crispy . . . iced drinks icy-cold! Pack **your** picnic in Tupperware!

TUPPERWARE *everywhere!*

Lunch box buddies . . . **Kit Kups,** set of 3 different sizes 95c, and **Pie Wedge** 39c each . . . add variety to lunch. Carry salads, pudding and fruits in Kit Kups. Pie Wedge protects pie, eliminates wrapping.

Tupperware keeps refrigerators and cupboards neat!

No unsightly half-used packages, torn wrappings. Store everything in neat, uniform air-tight, liquid-tight Tupperware . . . a glance shows the level of food in canisters. Tupperware saves space two ways: Patented Tupper Seal lets you store bowls, canisters and tumblers upside down or sideways. Tupperware containers come in many sizes — use the size to fit the need!

Tupperware Everywhere! 1950s catalog page demonstrates how Tupperware can keep your refrigerator and cupboards neat, and organize your next picnic.

Tupperware Ice Tups Set, six molds with handles and tray, 1950s-1960s.

$18-$20

Set came packaged with a small recipe folder.

Tupperware Pastry Sheet, with recipes and guide for pastry rolling, 1960s.

$18-$22

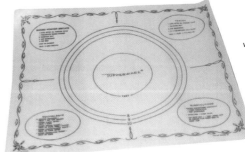

The 1970s version was printed in brown.

Tupperware Mustard and Catsup Dispensers, with lids, 1960s-1970s.

$12-$15

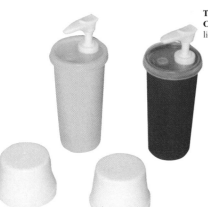

Tupperware All-In-One, combination sink strainer and refrigerator dish, 1950s.

$18-$25

Hard-to-find early Tupperware item.

Tupperware Colander, 1950s.

$12-$15

Tupperware Grid Top Colander, colander base with open net lid, 1960s.

$12-$15

Tupperware Sugar and Creamer Set, 1960s.

$12-$15

Earlier versions have rounder-shaped lids.

Tupperware Tumblers, 2 oz. "Midgets" with seals, set of six in pastel shades, 1950s-1960s.

$12-$15

Plastic Spice Rack, styrene plastic, non Tupperware, 1950s.

$12-$15

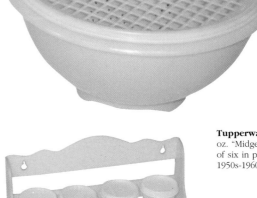

Tupperware Juicer, with storage container, 1960s-1970s.

$10-$12

TUPPERWARE *seals in food flavors*
Quick as a wink!

Easy to Apply . . .
Glide thumbs around.

Easy to Seal . . .
"Wink" seal up at edge.

Easy to Open . . . Lift edge . . . peel it back.

Now you can **save** that tempting coffee aroma . . . keep vegetables garden-fresh for days . . . turn leftovers into planovers. It's easy—and economical—with Tupperware!

When you seal Tupperware with the patented Tupper Seal, air whisks out . . . your food is virtually vacuum-packed.

Air-tight Tupperware locks moisture, air and insects *out,* food flavors and values *in.* You can stack Tupperware upside down or sideways — in the refrigerator, freezer and pantry—saving space as well as food!

And, remember, Tupperware will not crack, chip or break. It's made of Poly-T® material (especially blended formula of polyethylene) . . . flexible and durable . . . with a container for every food storage need.

See the magic Tupper Seal demonstrated at a Tupperware Home Party. You'll enjoy it!

For free booklet, "How to Guard Food Values", and information on being a Tupperware hostess or dealer, write . . .

TUPPERWARE HOME PARTIES INC., *Orlando, Florida*

184

Tupperware ad from *Good Housekeeping,* March, 1957. Model posing in the Tupperware test kitchen demonstrates how Tupperware seals in food flavors "Quick as a Wink!"

$2-$5

Tupperware Sprinkler Bottle, 1960s.

$15-$18

Tupperware Hamburger Press Set, with individual storage units, 1960s-1970s.

$10-$12

Chapter 33

Rubbermaid

In the late 1920s, two executives at the Wear-Ever division of the Aluminum Corporation of America, Horatio Ebert and Errett Grable, decided to purchase the Ohio-based Wooster Rubber Co. At the time Wooster Rubber was making toy balloons, gloves, and other items from latex rubber, but was failing to show much of a profit. The new ownership team helped revive the operation, but by the Depression years of the early 1930s it was paramount that new products be developed for the company to thrive.

At about the same time, James Caldwell, a rubber chemist formerly with the Seamless Rubber Co., had created an innovative-colored rubber dustpan and several other products. Initially turned down by retail outlets, since a rubber dustpan would sell at $1 versus the standard 39 cents, Caldwell set about marketing his dustpans door to door with encouraging results. This effort led to the first Rubbermaid store sales and drew the attention of Ebert and Grable at the Wooster Rubber Co. James Caldwell's expertise with rubber products and sales acumen fit closely into their need for growth. Combining Caldwell's Rubbermaid operation into the Wooster Rubber Co. proved beneficial to both parties.

By the 1930s, sales of dustpans, sink strainers, a molded steel-wool pad holder, and other household products became the primary source of revenue at the Wooster Rubber Co. A new manufacturing facility was opened, and in the 1940s new products, stressing innovation and quality such as a rubber-coated dish drainer led to increased sales. In the mid-1950s, items molded out of polyethylene starting with a sink strainer were added to the line. In 1957, Rubbermaid Inc. became the official company name. The 1960s, and later, saw the adoption of rotating lazy susans, food storage containers, and shelving systems, further expanding Rubbermaid sales and product categories.

Today, older Rubbermaid items appeal to many collectors of vintage kitchenware. For those who want to create a retro kitchen, a few Rubbermaid items from the 1950s help enhance the overall look, particularly when colors are matching. Recently, 1960s items in turquoise and other colors have shown strong buyer interest during Internet auctions.

Rubbermaid Shelf Kushions, "To beautify and protect your shelves permanently," boxed, 1950s.

$22-$25

Rubbermaid Steel Wool Holder, "Protects hands and nail polish," on card, 1950s.

$15-$18

Rubbermaid Stove Top Mats, "Provides extra cushioned work space while preparing meals," in package, 1950s,
small   **$25-$28**
large   **$25-$30**

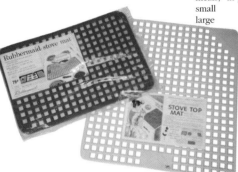

Rubbermaid Dustpan, 1950s.

$22-$25

This dustpan is an updated version of the original that launched the Rubbermaid line in the early 1930s. It's somewhat bulky due to the thickness of material.

Rubbermaid Sink Divider Mat, with card insert.

$22-$25

Blue is one of the less common kitchenware colors. The example shown is from Wark's Hardware in Valparaiso, Indiana. Its blue color may have kept it from finding a buyer in the 1950s, it was purchased at an auction of the store's remaining inventory in 2001.

Rubbermaid Colorful Coasters, set of eight, 1950s.

$15-$18

These coaster sets were miniatures of Rubbermaid Kar-Rugs, and were often used as promotion items.

Rubbermaid Drainer Tray, with label, 1960s.

$18-$22

The example shown was originally a promotion piece.

The modernized block Rubbermaid logo helps date this tray, pink color increases its value to collectors.

Rubbermaid Plate and Bowl Scraper, flexible rubber blade with rigid plastic end for scraping corners, on card, 1940s-1950s.

$22-$25

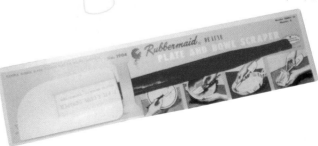

Rubbermaid Plate Rack, large size, "Keeps cupboards neat–Conserves space and provides handy access," 1940s-1950s.

$18-$22

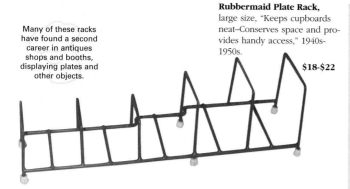

Rubbermaid Utensil Trays, polyethylene, blue with script logo, 1950s.

$12-$15

Rubbermaid Lazy Susan Canister Set, turquoise, styrene plastic, 1960s.

$25-$30

Rubbermaid Lazy Susan Canister Set, styrene plastic, 1970s.

$12-$18

Rubbermaid **DISH PAN**

No chipping, no clatter, and no wonder . . . they're

Rubbermaid dishpans

Pretty soft for dishes! Cushion your sink bowl, too, with a colorful, silent Rubbermaid dishpan. Breakage is all but impossible! Speeds daily dishwashing tasks. Handy for *many* household uses. From $1.69 to $1.98 in red, white, yellow or pink, wherever housewares are sold. Prices slightly higher in Canada.

For free folder showing all Rubbermaid products, write: *The Wooster Rubber Company,* **Department B-35, Wooster, Ohio.**

Guaranteed by Good Housekeeping

For more about Rubbermaid's polyethylene dishpans see opposite page.

131

Rubbermaid dishpan ad from *Better Homes and Gardens,* August, 1955.

Chapter 34

Plas-tex Corporation

The Plas-tex Corporation was a plastic housewares manufacturer headquartered on Military Ave. in Los Angeles, CA. Their 1940s-1950s product line consisted of picnic sets, pitchers, glasses, canister sets, and other kitchen and household items. In the mid-1950s, the product line was expanded to include polyethylene pails, wastebaskets, canisters, and a popular ice bucket. A number of Plas-tex products in the 1950s-1960s had distinctive flowing shapes, unlike those of other manufacturers.

Collectors today have shown interest in a number of early Plas-tex styrene items, particularly the Clospray sprinkler bottle, salt and pepper shakers, plastic sets, and unusual pieces. Plas-tex polyethylene products from the 1950s-1960s of most interest to collectors include ice buckets, canister sets, and a uniquely shaped mixing bowl set.

Plas-tex ad featuring Ice Buckets from *Good Housekeeping*, November, 1957. This polyethylene ice bucket, introduced in the mid-1950s, was well received by consumers. Many of its features were later copied by other manufacturers.

Plas-tex Bar-B-Que Set, set of four plates and cups, styrene plastic, boxed, 1950s.

$22-$25

Plas-tex Informal Dining Set, styrene plastic, "Colorful jumbo size eight piece set for informal dining," boxed, 1950s.

$22-$25

Plas-tex must have determined that Informal Dining and Bar-B-Ques had similar needs, the only difference was that one of the sets got a wavy-style handle.

Sometimes incorrectly described as pitchers, these boxy containers with a sliding lid over the spout were originally intended for use with soap flakes.

Plas-tex Soap Dispensers, styrene plastic, 1950s.

$15-$18 each

Plas-tex Cream and Sugar Set, styrene with hand-painted design, 1950s.

$15-$18

Art-Deco in appearance, this set was made in the 1950s, and is usually found without decoration. The sugar bowl pictured is missing its lid.

Plas-tex Canister Set, three-piece styrene plastic with clear lids, 1950s.

$18-$22

Plas-Tex Long John Tumbler Set, styrene plastic, "Six colorful tumblers for taller, cooler, better drinks and no metallic taste," boxed, 1950s.

$28-$35

Plas-tex Pitcher, styrene plastic, 2.5 qt. 1950s.

$18-$22

This pitcher was a companion piece to the Long John Tumbler Set.

Plas-tex Salt and Pepper Shaker Set, 1950s,

$15-$18 set

This mismatched set in two colors still goes well together.

Plas-tex Clospray Sprinkler Bottle, two-piece styrene body with removable sprinkler top and cork washer, 1950s. Add $3-$5 if it has a hand-painted decoration.

$18-$22

Plas-tex Measuring Spoons, styrene plastic, 1950s.

$15-$18

Another example of an added use for a current product, the nucleus of this dispenser is a salt and peppershaker body.

Plas-tex Cotton Dispenser, styrene plastic with hand-painted decoration, 1950s.

$20-$25

These polyethylene mixing bowls show wear after repeated use, decreasing the survival rate.

Plas-tex Mixing Bowls, polyethylene, for mixing and pouring, 1950s-1960s.

$18-$25 set

Plas-tex Canister Set, polyethylene, with molded in names on top handle, 1950s-1960s.

$20-$22

Curvaceous in shape, these canisters have a unique space-age modern look.

Plas-tex Canister Set, four pieces, polyethylene, 1950s-1960s.

$28-$35

BRIGHTEN EVERY ROOM LIGHTEN EVERY TASK!

Baking's a breeze with marvelous PLAS-TEX Mixing Bowls. 3-pc. set.......**2.98**

No clutter or clatter with PLAS-TEX trays. Giant Gad-getray, **1.79**; Cutlery tray, **.98**; Silvertray........**.79**

Protect your fine china. PLAS-TEX Dishpans, **1.98**; 4½-qt. Basin **.98**

KITCHEN

Snag-proof PLAS-TEX Laundry Baskets. Solid bottoms keep wash clean. Oval, **3.98** Round "bushel" Basket, **2.98**

Lifetime wastebaskets with sealing lids! PLAS-TEX 26-Qt. Basket, **3.98** Lid, **.98**; 40-qt., **4.98** Lid, **1.49**; 19-qt., **2.98** Lid, **.79**

SERVICE AREA

Rustproof and washable. Perfect for the bathroom. PLAS-TEX Oval Wastebasket, **1.98**; PLAS-TEX Round Wastebasket **1.49**

Safe for baby. PLAS-TEX Baby Bath. Exclusive non-slip bottom, **4.98**; Odor-sealing PLAS-TEX Diaper Pail **3.98**

BATHROOM

COLOR-STYLE YOUR HOME

THE BEST IN PLAS-TEX HOUSEWARES

POLYETHYLENE
— *The Miracle Material!*
Rustproof — Dentproof — Unbreakable
LASTS A LIFETIME!

Take your choice:

RED
PINK
TURQUOISE
YELLOW

PATIO

Lasts a lifetime. And a lid that really locks — it's dog-proof! 10 gal. PLAS-TEX G-Can, **7.98** 5 gal. G-Can **4.98**

Brand new pouring pail! It measures! It pours! It lightens chores! PLAS-TEX Pail, **2.98**

DINING

Beautiful PLAS-TEX brass-trimmed Fiberglas-insulated Ice Bucket. Keeps ice 18 hrs., **9.95**

Guaranteed by Good Housekeeping

Win a FREE PLAS-TEX ICE BUCKET
Register for drawing at your PLAS-TEX dealer. No purchase necessary!

Subject to Federal, state, and local regulations.

THE PLAS-TEX CORPORATION • Los Angeles 64, California

ASK FOR PLAS-TEX BY NAME at LEADING HARDWARE and DEPARTMENT STORES

LOOK FOR THIS TRADEMARK. PLAS-TEX YOUR GUIDE TO "THE BEST IN HOUSEWARES"

Plas-tex magazine ad from the late 1950s showing a sampling of their polyethylene products, "Brighten every room, lighten every task."

$2-$5

Chapter 35

Serving Dishes, Lazy Susans

Consumers eagerly took to the advantages of plastic serving dishes in the 1950s. Lighter in weight and more break resistant than their glass counterparts, they were also much lower in cost. Plastic dishes were easily transformed into a multitude of brightly colored shapes and styles, varying from simple bowls to exotic tropical and lotus leaf shapes. Some companies offered novel features like flip-top lids, finger holes, and multiple-piece sets with serving utensils. Of most interest to collectors today are sets with an original box having fun graphics. Any unusual shapes or features add to their appeal.

Lazy susans offer a simple, compact way of serving a selection of items. Popular with snacks, candies, or vegetables one server eliminates the need for a number of separate ones. Most rotate, hence the term "lazy," offering additional convenience and ease for the user. Plastic versions in the 1950s were lighter and easier to carry than comparable glass and wood units and are usually smaller in size. Many varieties exist and are usually harder to find than those made of other materials, since they couldn't withstand as much repeated use. Special features such as unusual colors or lids add to collector appeal.

Saturday Evening Post, November 11, 1961, with cover illustration by George Hughes. The serving line of a fancy dinner party is being invaded by a member of the younger set. The lady behind the table, obviously his mom, is doing her dignified best to ignore him.

$8-$10

Tele-Servers, Styrene plastic, set of four, server and tumbler sets, "For TV serving, handy, convenient," boxed, 1950s, APCO, Associated Plastic Corp., Chicago, IL.

$25-$28

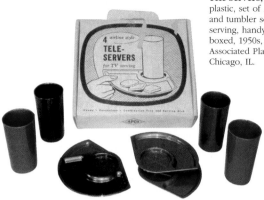

Coaster/Snack Dish, styrene plastic, set of three, 1950s, Federal Tool Corp., Chicago, IL.

$8-$10

Tropical Moon Coasters, set of eight, styrene plastic, "Not an ashtray," boxed, 1950s, Hoffman Industries Inc., Sinking Springs, PA.

$20-$22

Hi-Snack Plates, set of four, styrene plastic, "The plate that holds both glass and snacks in one hand, No juggling," boxed, 1950s, A Serv-Rite Product, Alexander & Wilson Co., Pasadena, CA.

$22-$25

Lazy Susan, styrene plastic, angular-shaped design in two-tone green, 1950s, Beacon Plastics.

$18-$22

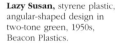

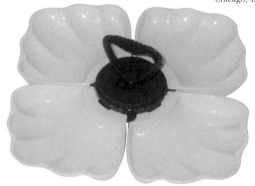

Deluxe Serving Tray, styrene plastic, large size in two-tone green with brown center, 1950s, Another Superlon Product, Superior Plastics, Chicago, IL.

$25-$28

Lazy Susan, styrene plastic, two-tone green, 1950s, Federal Tool Corp., Chicago, IL.

$15-$18

Deluxe Lazy Susan, large size in two tone green with clear section covers, 1950s, Federal Tool Corp., Chicago, IL.

$28-$35

Traymaster Deluxe Server, clear styrene plastic with metallic retractable lids, 1950s.

$22-$25

A Karoff Original, made in USA, finger-tip action opens "leaf" lids, which can be locked in position.

Leaf Server, styrene plastic with metal carrying handle and utensils, 1950s, A Karoff Original.

$18-$20

Lanai Salad Set, deluxe six pieces, styrene plastic with serving tongs, boxed, 1950s, Flex "BW" Ware.

$25-$28

California Fiesta Serving Set, six pieces, styrene plastic with serving tongs, "Ideal for salads, chips, popcorn, etc.," boxed, 1950s.

$28-$30

Serving Set, large bowl with eight small bowls, styrene plastic, 1950s, Burrite, The Burroughs Co., Los Angeles, CA.

$22-$25

Met-l-tone Salad Festival, seven pieces, styrene plastic, service for four, "Colorful with any interior," boxed, 1950s, Sterling Plastics, Union, NJ.

$25-$28

Salad Set, styrene plastic, nine-piece set with flower design, 1950s, Hoffman Industries Inc., Sinking Springs, PA.

$22-$25

Snack-Set, five pieces, melamine plastic, "For popcorn, salad, potato chips," with packaging card, 1960s-1970s, United Plastic Co., Townsend, MA.

$15-$18

Chapter 36

Kitchen Clocks

A wide selection of fun kitchen clocks were made from the 1940s to 1960s. The major companies, Telechron, General Electric, Sessions, Westclox, and others strove to outdo one another by continually introducing new, visually appealing models. Most were made primarily of plastic, however, other materials such as ceramics and metals were also used. Collectors find that a vintage clock makes an interesting accent piece with figural shapes or special designs appealing to many. The relatively few collectors concentrating solely on clocks allows ample opportunity to satisfy individual preferences. With kitchen clocks, style, color, and condition are important factors affecting value. Versions used in a display need not work, but top dollar is usually reserved for working examples.

General Electric Clock ad from *Woman's Day*, December, 1951.
$2-$5

Look! Six exciting new clocks!

New calendar alarm ... TELE-JOUR
... shows day and date automatically. **14.95***

New metal alarm ... TELECRAT
... with the rich gleam of gold-color metal. **6.98***

New luminous alarm ... DECOR
... a real decorator's delight in design. **7.98***

When minutes matter...

trust Telechron
ELECTRIC CLOCKS

Electric ... no winding, no noisy tick-tock

Accurate ... so dependable ... can't run fast or slow

Guaranteed ... written warranty with each clock

Smartly styled ... for every room in your home

New luminous alarm ... GRACEWOOD
Mahogany, maple or blond finishes. **8.98***

New shelf or wall clock ... TELECHOICE
Red, white, yellow or brown. **5.98***

New wall clock ... DIAMETER
... in brushed copper, brass or chrome finish. **14.95***

You'll find world-famous, dependable *Telechron®* electric timing in the finest clocks, clock-radios, ranges, defrosters and heat controls.

*Prices plus tax. Prices and specifications subject to change without notice. Telechron is a trademark for products of Telechron Department, General Electric Company, Ashland, Mass.

Telechron Clocks ad from *Saturday Evening Post*, 1950s, Telechron div. of the General Electric Co., Ashland, MA.

$2-$5

Telechron "Telechoice" Shelf or Wall Clock, styrene plastic with metallic waterfall ends, 1950s.

$35-$40

Telechron Kitchen Clock, styrene plastic with metallic wrap-around center sections, 1940s-1950s.

$45-$50

Telechron Kitchen Clock, styrene plastic with rounded front corners, 1950s.

$22-$25

Values of white kitchen clocks are usually 20-25% less than a comparable model in color.

Telechron Clock, styrene plastic with smaller rounded off square design, 1950s.

$22-$25

Telechron Clock, styrene plastic with rectangle shape, 1950s-1960s.

$22-$25

Telechron Clocks, styrene plastic, "floating" bubble clock design with an outer numerical band, 1950s, in yellow with black numerals.

$45-$50;

Telechron Clocks, styrene plastic, "floating" bubble clock design with an outer numerical band, 1950s, in red with white numerals.

$65-$75

Condition is important on this clock, white numerals on red version usually show wear.

General Electric Clock, styrene plastic, with perimeter scallop design, 1950s-1960s.

$22-$25

Telechron ad featuring a "floating" bubble clock design. from *Better Homes and Gardens*, October 1953, Telechron div. of General Electric Co.

Spartus clock, styrene plastic, with numeral "pods" protruding from center section, 1950s, Herold Products Co., Chicago, IL.

$40-$45

With kitchen clocks, unusual space-age designs in bright colors translate into increased value.

Westclox "Manor" Clock, styrene plastic in rectangular design, 1950s-1960s, Westclox, LaSalle, IL.

$22-$25

General Electric Clock, pink and white styrene with clear cover, 1950s.

$25-$28

Pink clocks usually command premium prices.

Westclox "Wallmate" Clock, smaller styrene plastic square design with round clock center, 1950s, Westclox, LaSalle, IL.

$22-$25

Sunbeam Clock, styrene plastic, round design with squared numerical backgrounds, 1960s, Sunbeam Products Co., Chicago, IL.

$12-$15

Little interest is shown for avocado clocks, designed to harmonize with the dark kitchen cabinets of the late 1960s.

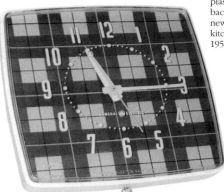

General Electric "Clansman" Clock, styrene plastic with plaid background design, "Lends new glamour to any kitchen's color scheme," 1950s.

$22-$25

Sessions Kitchen Clock, plastic teapot-shaped design, 1950s, Sessions Clock Co., Forrestville, CT.

$55-$60

Sunbeam "Kitchenette" Clock, styrene plastic, "Add beauty to your kitchen," in package, 1950s-1960s, Sunbeam Products Co.

$25-$28

Fanciful figural clocks are collector favorites, especially with bright colors.

Sessions Kitchen Clock, plastic "Pierre" chef-shaped design, 1950s, Sessions Clock Co.

$50-$55

Ceramic Kitchen Clock, designed by Russel Wright with General Electric movement, 1950s.

$65-$75

This hard-to-find clock was made in several glaze colors and is a companion product to Russel Wright dinnerware.

Seth Thomas Apple Clock, styrene plastic with painted leaves and stem, 1950s, Seth Thomas Clocks, div. of General Time Corp., Thomaston, CT.

$45-$55

United Pocket Watch Clock, plated brass housing with metal chain, 1950s.

$65-$75

This clock is a familiar favorite of mine, since an identical one hung in the family kitchen for more than 20 years.

Kit Cat Klock, styrene plastic, battery operated with moving eyes and tail, 1950s, California Clock Co., San Juan Capistrano, CA.

$35-$50

Originating in the 1950s, an electrified version of this clock is still being produced. Other varieties exist including a French Poodle, a Klocker Spaniel, and some with rhinestone decoration. Expect to pay a premium for unusual examples.

Westclox Kitchen Clock, styrene plastic with snowflake-pattern numerals and clear cover. 1950s, Westclox, a product of General Time Corp., LaSalle, IL.

$30-$35

Telechron "Advisor" Kitchen Clock, two-color styrene plastic with cut out numerals, 1950s.

$25-$28

Chapter 37

Salt & Pepper Shakers

T he seemingly unlimited variety of plastic salt and pepper shakers made enable collectors to
easily focus on subjects of interest or concentrate on certain types. Although the stature
and cost of vintage shakers have increased substantially from their dime store origin, they
can still be considered a sort of collectible bonbon, pleasant and enjoyable, but not particularly
rare. For collectors, boxed versions and fanciful designs increase interest with the use of wall
displays providing a typical way to showcase collections. For plastic salt and pepper shakers, the
emphasis remains on the fun with other collecting benefits an added bonus.

Salt & Pepper Shakers. Hundreds of different designs were produced over the
years and they make a fun collectible. A sampling is shown here neatly residing
in their own house-shaped display rack.

I made the display rack pictured above based on an Italian design. Readers are
encouraged to contact me if they want a similar display rack of their own. See
my contact information on the About the Author page.

Magic-Spray Salt & Pepper Servers, styrene plastic with push button mechanism, boxed, 1950s, Magii Products Inc., Rockford, IL.

$18-$20

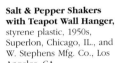

Cat and Dog Salt & Pepper Shakers, styrene plastic with painted details, promotional set from Ken-L Ration dog food, 1950s, marked F&F Tool and Die, Dayton, OH.

$25-$28

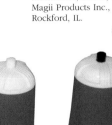

Salt & Pepper Shakers with Teapot Wall Hanger, styrene plastic, 1950s, Superlon, Chicago, IL., and W. Stephens Mfg. Co., Los Angeles, CA.

$22-$25 set

Egg-shaped Salt & Pepper Shakers, styrene plastic with clear base, with mailing carton, 1950s.

$18-$22

This set was a promotional offer from the Quaker Oats Co.

Penguin Pals Salt & Pepper Set, fluted glass body with plastic head and tuxedo, boxed, 1950s, D'Art Craftsman Corp., New York, NY.

$25-$28

Camel Salt & Pepper Shaker, styrene plastic with shaker "humps," 1950s.

$18-$20

Spicer-ette Dispenser, six compartments, styrene plastic, "Handy, compact, sprinkles or pours, Spice supply always visible," boxed, 1950s, Spicer-ette Co., San Francisco, CA.

$22-$25

Whimsical Character Salt & Pepper Shakers, styrene plastic with painted details, 1950s.

$18-$22

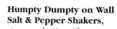

Matches canister set with design features of Federal Housewares, Chicago, IL.

Salt & Pepper Shakers, styrene plastic with diamond design, 1950s, unmarked.

$15-$18

Salt & Pepper Shaker Set, styrene plastic with wall hung, gazebo-like cage design, 1950s, Superlon, Chicago, IL. Add $8-$10 for earlier version with two color cage, bird and background mirror.

$18-$22

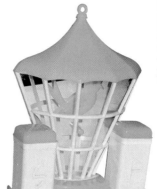

Humpty Dumpty on Wall Salt & Pepper Shakers, styrene plastic with contrasting color top, 1950s.

$25-$28

Pear Salt & Pepper Set, styrene plastic with painted details and holder, 1950s, made in USA.

$20-$22

Salt & Pepper Shakers, styrene plastic with contrasting lid and raised design S and P, 1950s, Burrite, Burroughs Mfg. Corp., Los Angeles, CA.

$15-$18

Pop Up Toaster Salt & Pepper Set, styrene plastic, bread slice shakers with toaster holder, boxed, 1950s, a Starke design.

$22-$25

Miniature Mixer Salt & Pepper Set, styrene plastic with detachable bowl for sugar, boxed 1950s.

$25-$28

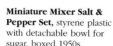

Kitten Salt & Pepper Shakers, styrene plastic, painted details, 1950s, add $5-$8 if plastic holder is included.

$15-$18

Serv-Rite Corn Salt & Pepper Shakers, two styrene plastic sets, boxed, 1950s, Royal Pacific Co., Los Angeles, CA.

$15-$18

Some have sticker on lid, "As seen on the Home Show with Arlene Francis."

Steri-lite Tongs and Shakers Set, styrene plastic, 1950s.

$30-$35

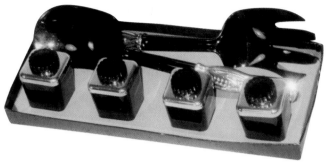

Bean Pot Salt & Pepper Set, styrene plastic, boxed, 1950s, "It's a honey," Bee Plastics Inc., Cambridge, MA.

$18-$20

Serv-Rite Range Set Salt & Pepper Shakers, styrene plastic with contrasting lid, boxed, 1950s.

$12-$15

Round Salt & Pepper Shakers, solid and clear styrene plastic, with flat bottoms, "Ideal for home, picnics, and seashore, Every smart hostess will use them," boxed, 1950s, Jiggs/Penny.

$15-$18

Stanley Ball Point Salt & Pepper Shakers, clear and solid styrene plastic with missile-shaped design, boxed, 1950s, Stanley Home Products Co.

$12-$15

Chapter 38

Canister Sets

P lastic canister sets, usually consisting of separate flour, sugar, coffee, and tea containers first became popular in the late 1940s. The advantages of bright colors, easily cleaned rounded corners, and low cost quickly made them preferable over wood, metal, or glass versions. Canister sets helped establish plastics in the kitchens of America and led to the acceptance of other products. Collectors usually look for sets that match their other collectibles or fit a chosen color scheme. Condition is important with mint examples considerably more desirable than those showing wear.

Lustro-Ware Sales Pamphlet, "Brightens kitchens, Lightens work," 1950s.

$30-$35

Pamphlet also provides a color availability chart for the various products.

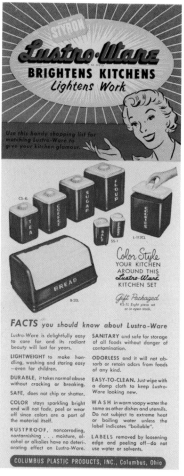

Popular Mechanics, October 1953, with cover illustration by Korta. Cover shows a 1950s couple in perfect harmony, he heads to the shop (in shirt and tie) and she goes to the kitchen. **$6-$8**

Canister Set, four-piece styrene plastic, rectangular in turquoise with white lids and embossed metallic labels. 1950s-1960s, Beacon Plastics.

$18-$22

Canister Set, four-piece styrene plastic, rounded corner design in pink and gray with integral handle lids and block lettering, 1950s, Burrite, Burroughs Mfg. Co., Los Angeles, CA.

$28-$35

This unmarked set is an unusual find with its original box.

Canister Set, three-piece styrene plastic, "The smart set for smart kitchens. The first and only canister set with a window, a feature to gladden any woman's heart," boxed, 1950s, Janetware Plastic Products, Aurora, IL.

$40-$45

Plastic Canister/Container, styrene plastic in pink and gray with lid, 1950s, Gitsware, Gits Molding Corp., Chicago, IL.

$12-$15

Salt & Pepper with Sugar Container, three-piece styrene plastic set with hand-painted flower decoration, 1950s, Plastic Novelties Inc., Los Angeles, CA.

$22-$25

Cookie Canister, red styrene plastic with white lid and lettering, 1950s.

$18-$22

Unmarked with design features of Federal Housewares, Chicago, IL.

The copper metallic lids and kitchen decoration help separate this set from the ordinary.

Canister Set, four-piece styrene plastic, rounded-corner design in metallic copper and yellow, with integral handle lids and decoration, 1950s-1960s, Burrite, Burroughs Mfg. Co., Los Angeles, CA.

$35-$40

Popeil Canister Set, three-piece styrene plastic with white lids, 16 oz., 32 oz., and 64 oz., with labels, 1950s, Popeil Bros., Chicago, IL.

$30-$35

Popeil Canister Set, three pieces, styrene plastic with clear lids and leaf design, 1950s, Popeil Bros.

$22-$25

Bread Box, styrene plastic, 1950s, Burrite, Burroughs Mfg. Co.

$15-$18

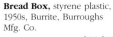

Canister Set, four pieces, styrene plastic, rounded-corner design in yellow with integral handle lids and flower decal, 1950s, Burrite, Burroughs Mfg. Co.

$28-$35

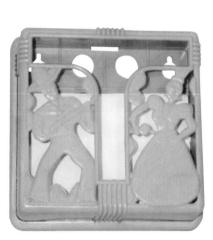

Canister/Cookie Jar, styrene plastic, rounded design with lid, 1950s, Burrite, The Burroughs Mfg. Co.

$22-$25

Napkin Holder, two pieces, styrene plastic with molded festive musician figures, 1940s-1950s.

$30-$35

Canister Set, four pieces, styrene plastic with embossed lettering, 1950s-1960s, Lustro-Ware, Columbus Plastic Products Co., Columbus, OH.

$25-$28

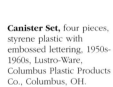

Canister Set, four pieces, styrene plastic, rounded-corner design in pink with gray knobs and kitchen decorations, 1950s-1960s, Burrite, Burroughs Mfg. Co., Los Angeles, CA.

$28-$35

Ice Bucket, styrene plastic with handle, lid and flower decoration, 1950s, Trans Spec Corp., Cleveland, OH.

$18-$22

Bibliography

Arnold, Lionel K. *Introduction to Plastics.* Ames, IA : The Iowa State University Press, 1968.

Bercovici, Ellen; Bryson, Bobbie Zucker; Gillham, Deborah. *Collectibles for the Kitchen, Bath and Beyond.* Iola ,WI : Krause Publications, 2001.

Celehar, Jane H. *Kitchens and Gadgets, 1920-1950.* Radnor, PA : Wallace–Homestead, 1982.

Cohn, Jan. *Covers of the Saturday Evening Post.* New York, NY : Smithmark Publishers, 1998.

Fenichell, Stephen. *Plastic, The Making of a Synthetic Century.* New York, NY : Harper Collins Publishers, Inc., 1996.

Franklin, Linda Campbell. *300 Years of Kitchen Collectibles.* Iola, WI : Krause Publications, 2001.

Goldberg, Michael J. *Collectible Plastic Kitchenware and Dinnerware.* Atglen, PA : Schiffer Publishing, Ltd., 1995.

Goldberg, Michael J. *Groovy Kitchen Designs for Collectors, 1935–1965.* Atglen, PA : Schiffer Publishing, Ltd., 1996.

Hine, Thomas. *Populuxe.* New York, NY : Borzoi Books, 1986.

Lifshey, Earl. *The Housewares Story.* Chicago, IL : The National Housewares Manufacturers Association, 1973.

Mantranga, Victoria Kasuba. *America at Home, A Cellibration of Twentieth–Century Housewares.* Rosemont, IL : The National Housewares Manufacturers Association, 1997.

Mauzy, Barbara E. *The Complete Book of Kitchen Collecting.* Atglen, PA : Schiffer Publishing, Ltd., 1997.

McDaniel, Patricia. *Drugstore Collectibles.* Radnor, PA : Wallace – Homestead, 1996.

Sparke, Penny. *The Plastics Age.* Woodstock, NY : The Overlook Press, 1993.

Stoneback, Diane. *Kitchen Collectibles, The Essential Buyer's Guide.* Radnor, PA : Wallace–Homestead, 1994.

Ward, Pete. Fantastic Plastic, *The Kitsch Collector's Guide.* Edison, NJ : Chartwell Books, 1997.

Index

About the Author

Here I am today, trying out a 1950s comic barbecue apron.

Brian S. Alexander was born in Peru, Indiana and raised in Michigan City, Indiana. He studied Interdisciplinary Engineering at Purdue University where he invented and designed products in his spare time. This effort produced a patent for a baton twirling doll, a game, and a pet-rock-like novelty product, "Clothing for Telephones," that was featured in several newspaper articles. After graduating from Purdue he worked as a design engineer and a consultant for a medical products company, where he was awarded two more patents.

He returned to college and received a master's degree in Architecture from the Illinois Institute of Technology. While continuing his studies he was involved in several interim jobs and projects. A singer songwriter for many years, he released "Bandazzle," a combined record album and game that was recommended by Billboard magazine. He worked at a job in customer service in Evanston, IL with Tina Fey, who later went on to be featured on Saturday Night Live. He also worked for Murphy/Jahn Architects in Chicago. He presently works in architecture and has homes in Evanston, IL and Michigan City, IN.

A dedicated James Dean fan, with whom he shares a similar birthday and county origin, in the 1990s he set out to redecorate his home in the style of the 1950s. This exposed him to all types of gadgets and household items of the period. His interests as a collector took him to over 200 antique malls, shops, flea markets, and shows from Columbus, Ohio to Des Moines, Iowa and on more than a few Internet excursions. As his collections grew, he thought that someday he might write a book on the subject. In 2001, Eric Zorn at the Chicago Tribune started a motivational program where individuals start working on one of their long put-off "someday projects," and Brian signed up. After over two years of work you are holding the results in your hands. Contact Brian at Spiffykitchen@hotmail.com.

A photo showing myself (small boy in the middle) experiencing the 1950s firsthand. Also in the picture are sister Jody, brothers Greg, Doug, and father Ramon. In the background is our family wagon, a red 1955 Chevy Nomad, that Ramon Alexander purchased new off the showroom floor in Portland, Indiana. It served the dual purpose of wagon and stylishness for many years, and is still family owned.